Access to History

General Editor: Keith Randell

Sweden and the Baltic 1523–1721

Andrina Stiles

Hodder & Stoughton

LONDON SYDNEY AUCKLAND

The cover illustration shows a portrait of Gustavus Adolphus
(courtesy Livrustkammaren, Stockholm)

Other titles in the series:

Luther and the German Reformation, 1517–55   ISBN 0 340 51808 1
Keith Randell

Henry VIII and the Government of England   ISBN 0 340 55325 1
Keith Randell

Henry VII   ISBN 0 340 53801 5
Caroline Rogers

Charles V: Ruler, Dynast and Defender of the Faith   ISBN 0 340 53558 X
Stewart Macdonald

John Calvin and the Later Reformation   ISBN 0 340 52940 7
Keith Randell

The Catholic and Counter Reformations   ISBN 0 340 53495 8
Keith Randell

British Library Cataloguing in Publication Data
Stiles, Andrina
    Sweden and the Baltic, 1523–1721.
    – (Access to history)
    I. Title   II. Series
    948.5
    ISBN 0 340 546441

First published 1992

© 1992 Andrina Stiles

Typeset by Wearside Tradespools, Boldon, Tyne and Wear
Printed in Great Britain for the educational publishing division of Hodder & Stoughton
Ltd, Mill Road, Dunton Green, Sevenoaks, Kent by Page Bros Ltd, Norwich

5 Domestic Affairs

Any account of Gustavus's reign which concentrated solely on foreign affairs and omitted his substantial domestic achievements would be one-sided and incomplete.

a) The Accession Charter of 1612

Gustavus Adolphus spent the first few months of his reign bargaining with the nobility. The Succession Pact of 1604 had decreed that if Charles IX died while his son was still under age, the government was to be carried on by a Council of Regency until Gustavus reached his eighteenth birthday. Full control of the country was not to be handed over to him for a further six years after that. There was widespread support in the country for the sentiments of a contemporary pamphleteer that Sweden must at all costs be preserved 'from such another bloody and oppressive reign' as that of the late king. One way to ensure this was to curb the power of the crown. The result was the Accession Charter of 1 January 1612. In return for dispensing with the terms of the Succession Pact of 1604 and allowing the young king to enjoy full political control immediately, 'seeing that in him God . . . has made up in understanding what he lacks in years', the *råd* was able to impose a number of conditions. These placed substantial limitations on royal freedom of action, to the advantage of the nobility in general and of the higher nobility in particular.

The king had to promise to govern according to the constitution and the rule of law. All members of the *råd* and all senior government officials had to be 'nobles of Swedish birth'. There were to be no more of the 'low-born secretaries' or ennobled foreigners employed as had been the case in earlier reigns. The constitutional importance of the *råd* was reaffirmed. Its consent had to be obtained for the making of new laws, for major foreign policy decisions, and for summoning the *riksdag*. For the next half century Gustavus Adolphus's Accession Charter replaced the royal absolutism of Charles IX with 'aristocratic constitutionalism', while the appointment of Axel Oxenstierna as Chancellor in 1612 ushered in a new era of peaceful and fruitful cooperation between the nobility and the crown.

In addition, Lutheranism was confirmed by the Charter as the state religion, and all state officials from the sovereign downwards had henceforward to profess and maintain its faith. There was to be no toleration for non-Lutherans. This was made very clear six years later when all catholics were ordered to leave the country.

b) Domestic Reforms

i) The Administration

In a speech to the *riksdag* in August 1617 at the end of the war with

Muscovy (see page 46), Gustavus Adolphus gave notice of a programme of domestic reforms:

1 The peace affords us the opportunity once more to establish that good order and those good laws which the country formerly enjoyed, but which of late have been much in abeyance and through these long continued wars, as it were, forgotten. The
5 laws and statutes we have are indeed good; but by long misrule have fallen quite out of use. Courts are indeed held, in every province and county, but it is little justice the commonalty get from them, whence it comes that lawlessness prevails over law and right. Have I not set my face against such things? Indeed, as
10 God is my witness, I have done what I could. By Proclamations and beneficial Ordinances, I have as it were raised the law from the dead.

The resurrection of the law to which Gustavus referred was only the first step in a total reconstruction of the administration.

In 1611 the machinery of government had changed little since 1560. It remained a very primitive affair, and still very much the personal concern of the king. Official letters and documents were drafted and written by a few secretaries acting on the king's instructions: royal revenues were collected and paid in by the king's bailiffs from time to time at whatever place the court happened to be. All was ill-organised and uncoordinated. There was no central court of justice – the courts still followed the king around and he personally heard all appeals – and the *råd* (the Council of State) met only irregularly.

By 1626 the picture had altered completely. The changes made in the intervening years were based on the delegation of royal authority, the centralisation of government and a modernisation of its procedures.

The reform of justice had been effected by a series of Judicature Ordinances in 1614 and 1615. These set up a Supreme Court under the control of the High Steward, and appointed a bench of 13 judges, drawn from nobles and commoners, whose decisions were to be arrived at by majority vote. Sessions, which would last for five months at a time, were to be permanently centred on Stockholm – the days of the roving court following the king were over. The foundations for the development of case law were laid by ordering the court to keep careful records of all decisions made. Law became a respectable and responsible profession and began to attract recruits, especially once educational opportunities had been improved (see page 60).

The Treasury was overhauled and modernised by the Exchequer Ordinance of 1618. A new Treasury Board was established whose decisions were to be collective and which was to keep accurate records and to follow strict procedural regulations. A central system of accounting and auditing was set up, and further safeguards were

CHAPTER 4

Sweden as a Great Power 1632–60

1 Christina 1632–54

a) Oxenstierna and the Regency 1632–44

Gustavus Adolphus's heir was his six-year-old daughter and only child, Christina. There was no dispute over the succession, for the *riksdag* had agreed in 1604 that a woman could inherit the throne if, as here, there were no direct male heir. Immediately after Gustavus's death, the *råd* took temporary control of the government in Sweden while Axel Oxenstierna, who was in Germany, looked after Swedish interests there. Discussions about the form the regency should take led eventually to the adoption of a plan put forward by Oxenstierna.

Only eight days after the battle of Lützen, he had sent back from Germany a proposed constitution, known as the Form of Government. Although it followed along the lines of existing administrative practice, it placed additional emphasis on the authority of the high aristocracy. It provided that only in an emergency would the *riksdag* be convened and even a full meeting of the 24 members of the *råd* would not usually be called to discuss policy. Decisions would normally be left to the heads of the five colleges, or government departments, (the chancery, treasury, high court, the admiralty and the college of war) who might occasionally consult, if they considered it necessary, with a select committee of nobles, bishops and burghers. These five chief officers of state, all members of the *råd*, would form the Regency Council of which Axel Oxenstierna, the chancellor, would be chairman. As his brother and a cousin were two of the other chief officers, the Oxenstierna family were assured of a firm hold on the government. They maintained it for over a decade, until Christina came of age in 1544.

The Form of Government has been described as 'a programme for oligarchal rule under cover of the sovereign's name', and as a further limitation of royal power in favour of 'noble constitutionalism', a process begun by the Accession Charter of 1612 (see page 57). There had been a number of drafts of the document in circulation before Gustavus's death, but whether he saw and approved this particular one as the best form of government in the event of his death is uncertain. Oxenstierna certainly informed the *råd* that he had, but the chancellor's detractors at that time and since have suggested otherwise. Some, including one modern historian, think that he wrote it himself, and then put it forward in the late king's name in order to assure his own position and to advance his family's ambitions. The matter remains one of conjecture for there is not enough evidence available to determine which view is the right one.

The proposals for the Regency were reluctantly accepted by the *riksdag* in 1634. An oligarchy had been established. There was nobody to speak up for the crown – the queen was much too young to be aware of what was happening, and the extremely neurotic Queen Mother was specifically excluded from the Regency as unfitted for government.

b) Oxenstierna and the War in Germany

In 1633 Oxenstierna, at the age of 50, enjoyed a very considerable prestige in Europe. Since 1626 he had very efficiently administered first the Swedish wartime conquests in Poland and Prussia, and then Gustavus's more recent acquisitions in Germany. Although he was no soldier either by experience or inclination, at the end of 1632 he found himself forced into the position of Gustavus's *de facto* successor in Germany and in charge of military operations there. He was also responsible for deciding foreign policy, but in that field at least he was well experienced. At the same time he remained head of the Regency government at home, not simply in name but in reality. As a result he was continually required to make decisions on domestic issues as well as to conduct the war. His voluminous correspondence over the next decade shows that he was kept extremely busy by the demands of his dual role.

His immediate aim in Germany was to bring Swedish participation in the war to an end, but only with honour and only with suitable 'satisfaction' to recompense Sweden for her great expenditure of men and materials. It was a difficult and delicate situation with which he was faced. The cost of the war was proving to be enormous – military expenditure in 1630–1 had been ten times as much as Sweden's ordinary revenue for that year. Retrenchment was essential. But the 100,000 soldiers still in Swedish service in Germany had to be paid. They could no longer live off newly conquered land, as they had in the early days of the war. Some means must be found to shift the financial, and at least part of the military, burden of the war on to other shoulders, without jeopardising Sweden's rights to eventual 'satisfaction'.

Early in 1633 Oxenstierna sent home to the Regency Council a memorandum setting out his plans for Germany. He favoured disbanding part of the main army, 90 per cent of which was now made up of mercenaries, and using the remainder to garrison a number of strategically important places in south and west Germany. This would save money. The élite native Swedish troops would be permanently stationed in north Germany, in Swedish-held Pomerania and Prussia. There they would provide a strong defensive barrier against any Polish or Habsburg attempts to use the Baltic ports as bases from which to invade Sweden. He also proposed setting up a defensive league or confederation of friendly German princes under Swedish control. Such a league would not only act as a buffer against Habsburg aggression but would provide money to pay for the conduct of the war and produce suitable 'satisfaction' for Sweden at the end of it. Just before his death Gustavus had written to Oxenstierna outlining a similar plan, and:

1 Charging the Chancellor by gentle means to try to induce them [the princes] to join together in defence of their welfare and of the common cause and to find means to turn their resolve into action . . . and use every effort to secure these points:
5 1 To induce them to break away from the Emperor . . . and come under the direction and protection of His Majesty.
   2 To join together to prosecute the war.
   3 To devise means whereby the armies which His Majesty has planned and ordered may be supported and discipline pre-
10 served.

In April 1633 Oxenstierna presided over a meeting of protestant princes at which the League of Heilbronn was formed. The League was weakened from the start by the absence from it of the important states of Brandenburg and Saxony. One historian has described it as no more than 'a rump of Swedish puppets'. They certainly raised no difficulties about making the decisions that Oxenstierna wanted. In return for Swedish military assistance past and present the princes agreed:

1 To help the Swedish crown to keep possession of those enemy lands within the Empire which it already occupies until the war is over and a proper satisfaction is afforded . . .

The princes also agreed to maintain a substantial army, and to pay off the arrears owed to Swedish troops already serving in Germany. This would have solved Oxenstierna's most pressing problem – how to pay his men – but unfortunately these arrears proved to be much greater than expected, stretching back over several years. While efforts were being made to find out exactly how much was owing, the unpaid soldiers in south Germany mutinied. Oxenstierna dealt with the immediate problem there by giving local commanders the right to levy contributions directly from specified areas. This was interpreted by the soldiers as a 'licence to plunder', and they soon took to exacting their wages for themselves from the local population without reference to their officers. After these initial difficulties had been resolved, pay-ments made by the League of Heilbronn reduced the cost of the war to Sweden dramatically from just under three million daler in 1630 to less than 130,000 daler in 1633. No wonder Oxenstierna wrote to his brother, 'our forefathers and we have never carried on any war with greater ease to ourselves'. As one Swedish historian has remarked, it was 'war by proxy' which, as long as the League lasted, was extremely successful from the Swedish point of view.

In February 1634 Oxenstierna held a meeting of all the protestant princes of the Empire in the hope of strengthening the League by incorporating into it all those non-catholic states which were still holding aloof. He also hoped to persuade the princes to nominate those German territories which Sweden would be given as 'satisfaction' at the end of the war. In both these aspirations he was disappointed. The talks quickly became deadlocked. Nevertheless, in July the Swedes and their Heilbronn allies took the field and launched attacks in Bohemia and Bavaria. At first all went well, but in September 1634 outside the protestant city of Nördlingen the Swedes suffered a crushing defeat, leaving almost half their army dead on the field. Oxenstierna was deeply dispirited by the news – so much so that he suffered the second sleepless night of his life. Uncharacteristically, he seemed on the point of giving up. 'I will struggle no longer', he wrote, 'but drift where the tide may take me'. In Sweden, the Regency Council expressed fierce criticism of the conduct of the war, while in Germany, the battle of Nördlingen destroyed the legend of Swedish military invincibility and with it the viability of the League of Heilbronn. The idea of a 'corpus', a Swedish-dominated German alliance, seemed suddenly a much less attractive proposition to the princes. Three months later most of Sweden's German allies were negotiating for peace with the Emperor.

To add to Oxenstierna's difficulties, the 1629 Polish truce was due to expire in 1635. In order to prevent a renewal of hostilities with Poland, the Regents surrendered the valuable Prussian tolls as the price of a new 26 year truce. 'A disastrous price', grumbled Oxenstierna, for whom finding money to pay the army had again become a pressing problem. In August 1635 he himself was taken prisoner near Magdeburg by mutinous mercenaries demanding their pay and threatening to invade Sweden at the end of the war if they had not received their arrears before then. He managed to make an undignified escape, but from this moment the acquisition of money for 'the contentment of the soldiery' took its place beside security and 'satisfaction' as an essential Swedish war aim.

* At home the government continued to take a gloomy view of the situation amidst growing cries of 'Peace at any price'; 'What good does it do to acquire many lands and spend all our money on them?'; or 'It is intolerable to go on fighting a war in which we have no interest'. The members of the Regency Council decided that every effort should be made to bring Swedish involvement in Germany to an end, and agreed that:

1 While it was desirable that suitable satisfaction (preferably in the form of territory) should be obtained, if he [Oxenstierna] cannot get that, he should try by every means consistent with reputation and safety to extricate himself from the German business.

In the face of this strong opposition to continued military action and now desperate for money, Oxenstierna began to consider the possibility of a negotiated peace with the Habsburg Emperor. An approach to Saxony to act as mediator proved fruitless. As no other avenue to an honourable peace presented itself to Oxenstierna, he decided that the only alternative was to find an ally willing to provide the financial support needed to keep Sweden in the war. He accordingly began negotiations with France which had entered the war as an enemy of the Habsburgs in 1635. There were difficulties involved in arriving at an agreement, for Oxenstierna had deep-rooted suspicions of the French:

1 I have had experience of their tricks in former years. They commit hostile acts against us under a mask of friendship. But necessity is a great argument, and for a handful of gold one must often sacrifice reputation.

After much prevarication and quibbling over terms on Oxenstierna's part, a Franco-Swedish treaty was finally ratified in 1638. This bound both parties not to make a separate peace for the next three years, and provided Sweden with what Oxenstierna disparagingly, and ungratefully, called 'a squirt of money' – in other words, the subsidies of which Sweden had such urgent need. Like Gustavus before him, Oxenstierna had found in catholic France a paymaster for the Swedish troops in Germany. This time, however, Sweden was not just taking the money, but was committed to fighting alongside France in a common cause – it was the end of any last lingering pretence that Sweden was leading a protestant crusade. Oxenstierna was not concerned about this aspect as he had never believed religion to be the most significant element in the war in Germany (see page 56). What was important to him was that Sweden should do well out of any final peace settlement and, for that to happen, she must be on the winning side at the end of the war. An alliance with France seemed the best way of ensuring that this would be the case.

French gold transformed the situation in Germany for Oxenstierna. With money in their pockets the Swedish armies embarked on a series of successful campaigns. Once again the capture of Vienna seemed within the bounds of possibility. In 1641 the French treaty was renewed. By it, in return for the payment of subsidies at an increased rate, the Regents committed Sweden to continue to fight alongside France as long as the war should last.

c) Interlude in Denmark 1643–5

In 1643 relations between Sweden and Denmark were again bad. There had been more trouble over the Sound dues and over Danish involvement in a scandal involving the flight of the Queen Mother from

Sweden. The Danes felt threatened by Swedish expansion in the Baltic and in Germany, while the Regents in Stockholm suspected Denmark of evil intentions towards them.

In the summer of 1643, without any warning, Oxenstierna ordered the Swedish army to leave Moravia, after they had just won a substantial victory in the second battle of Breitenfeld, and to march towards the Baltic. They entered Jutland from the south early in 1644, and soon afterwards Skåne and Halland were attacked and ravaged by an army led by Oxenstierna's son-in-law. After much haggling over terms, a peace treaty was signed in 1645. By it Denmark ceded Gotland and Ösel, her naval bases in the eastern Baltic, and the two Norwegian frontier provinces of Jämtland and Härjedalen, long coveted by Sweden. In addition, in order to guarantee her exemption from all Sound dues, Sweden was to occupy Halland for 30 years, giving her a much improved access to the west (see the map on page 9). It was a very satisfactory outcome for Sweden to a short and comparatively inexpensive war. The humiliating defeat of Denmark had overturned the balance of power in the Baltic. Sweden no longer needed to worry about the possibility of encirclement by Denmark. The position was now reversed, and it was Denmark which was at risk from Sweden as

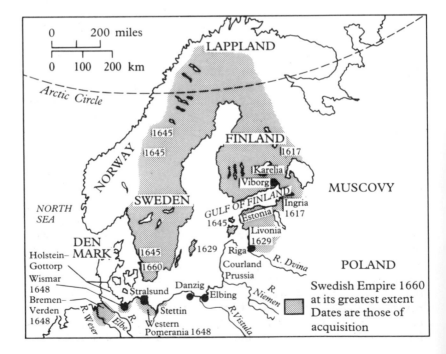

never before. Some Swedish historians regard the successful conclusion of this enterprise as the high point of Oxenstierna's whole career – a moment full of honour in which he was personally rewarded by the queen with lands and money, and publicly acclaimed by her as the faithful servant of his country and a man of 'pre-eminent skill and many great qualities'. Never again was their relationship to be so cordial for, as one historian has pointed out, this meeting in 1645 proved to be for Oxenstierna 'the last which was sweetened to him by the gratitude of the daughter of the great Gustavus'.

d) End of the War in Germany

In the last three years of the war Swedish forces advanced, retreated and advanced again in a series of inconclusive campaigns across Bavaria and Bohemia. When the fighting finally ended in November 1648 the Swedes were besieging Prague, the city where the Thirty Years' War had begun a generation earlier. As Oxenstierna had hoped, Sweden did finish the war on the winning side and, as he had planned, she was well provided for in the peace settlement. She obtained a large area of western Pomerania, including Stralsund and the port of Stettin; the port of Wismar in Mecklenburg; and the bishoprics of Bremen and Verden. After so much effort these gains might seem small in terms of area, but each brought economic, strategic or political advantage to Sweden. They gave her control of the mouths of three great German rivers, the Oder, the Elbe and the Weser, which flow into the Baltic. These important waterways gave access to the north German hinterland and opened up opportunities for Swedish middlemen to benefit from Baltic trade with the west. Pomerania, Wismar and Bremem-Verden were all well placed to provide bases from which to counter potential Habsburg attacks against the Swedish mainland, while Wismar and Bremen-Verden provided bases from which Sweden could threaten Denmark with invasion from the south (see the map on page 72). Oxenstierna had obtained in reasonable measure what he, and Gustavus before him, had wanted – satisfaction and security.

As the possessor now of colonies, however small or few in number, Sweden had become an imperial power, with importance beyond her own frontiers. Her new German territories were held as fiefs of the Habsburg Empire. Their scattered nature extended her political in-fluence over a wide area of Germany, especially as they brought with them the right to representation in the local assemblies. As one of the guarantors of the treaty which ended the war, the Peace of Westphalia, her international reputation was certain to increase, for it was inevitable that this appointment would involve her in diplomatic affairs well beyond the Baltic and northern Germany. By the end of 1648 she could no longer be classed as an insignificant and unregarded country of the far north. She had moved into the mainstream of European affairs as an acknowledged member of that select group, the major powers. Although she had not yet reached the limits of her territorial expansion – this was to come in 1660 – she was already the most powerful protestant state in Europe and possessed an enviable military reputation.

e) Sweden 1648–54

During the war the Regents had continued the policy of alienation – that is disposing of crown lands and revenues for ready cash. If the crown sold, donated or pawned the land or the taxes of a district to a noble, he gained the right to collect the taxes of the hitherto free crown peasants living there. It was also generally assumed – at least by the nobility – that he gained the same feudal rights over the newly acquired crown peasants as he already enjoyed over his own. With the alienation of so much land the number of free peasants declined sharply, reducing their social and economic status and their importance as the peasant estate in the *riksdag*. There were peasant protests against these abuses long before the end of the war, although the dissatisfaction did not come to a head until the meeting of the *riksdag* in 1650 (see page 76).

Alienation disturbed the balance of landownership between crown, nobility and peasants (see the Table of Changes in Landownership on page 18) with very serious implications for the long-term economy of the country. As more and more land fell into noble hands, it became *frälse* (exempt from tax), until by 1654 only about 28 per cent of all land was producing tax revenue. Each year the government found it more and more difficult to make ends meet without selling yet more land. The indirect taxation, customs dues and tolls on which the government increasingly relied, brought in disappointing sums. It was in an attempt to improve the situation that Axel Oxenstierna established a new government department, the college of commerce, to develop 'the exceeding rare and precious harbours in the Baltic . . . asking only wise exploitation to benefit the inhabitants of Sweden'. After 1648 Sweden controlled every major port on the Baltic except Lübeck, Königsberg and Danzig, and every river estuary from the Neva to the Weser except the Vistula. Oxenstierna believed that all these ports and waterways could produce a fortune in tolls if the trade through them was carefully encouraged. However, despite his urgings, disappointingly little was achieved at this time.

f) Queen Christina

In the course of the last three centuries historians and others have written at length about Queen Christina. They have analysed her complex and contradictory character and condemned or excused her remarkable, not to say sensational career. She remains, however, a strange, unhappy and rather pathetic figure whose appearance and behaviour shocked contemporary society.

Her inheritance was not good – there was insanity on both sides of the family – and this, coupled with a lonely and difficult childhood, produced an unpredictable and emotional young woman prone to psychosomatic illnesses. She was educated, in accordance with her father's instructions, in the same way as a male heir would have been. She proved to be extremely intelligent and followed with enthusiasm a very demanding academic course of study in addition to learning music and dancing. She was also devoted to outdoor pursuits, becoming an expert horsewoman and an excellent shot. She was extremely fond of hunting, often spending eight or nine hours at a time in the saddle. In an intended compliment, but which with hindsight reads more as a portent, Axel Oxenstierna described her to the *råd* as being, at the age of 14, 'not like a female but courageous and with a good understanding so that if she escape corruption she will answer every hope'. She was to disappoint him.

Christina was no beauty although her vivacity made up for the rather heavy features and prominent eyes inherited from her father. Throughout her life she spent little time on her appearance, and her clothes seem from contemporary accounts to have been not only untidy but often torn and dirty. Even in official portraits her clothes look shabby. As a young woman she freqently wore men's shoes and a man's coat over a long dress, but as time went by her costume and appearance became increasingly masculine. 'Her voice and manner of speaking, her walk, her style, her ways are all quite masculine . . . Unless one were close to her, one would take her for a man', wrote an impartial observer who knew her well, in the last year of her reign. 'There is nothing feminine about her except her sex' he added. If her sex was undisputed, her sexuality remains unclear. That she had at least one long-standing lesbian relationship appears certain; but equally certain is that she fell passionately in love with a least one man, and it is probable that she had affairs with a number of others. In her loves, as in the rest of her life, she remains as enigmatic as ever.

It had been expected of her since childhood that she would marry her cousin, Charles Gustavus of Zweibrücken (see the family tree on page 134) and so provide a Vasa heir to the throne. Considerable pressure was put on her to do so, but in 1649 she finally told the *riksdag* 'It is impossible for me to marry. Such is the nature of the case. I cannot give my reasons but my heart is not in it.'

* There is some evidence that in 1649 Christina was already considering abdication. However, she possessed a very strong sense of family loyalty, and before making any announcement she needed to be sure that the succession was secured in such a way as to keep the Vasa dynasty on the throne. Charles had to be accepted as the most suitable person to be her heir, even if he were not her husband (he had no hereditary right to the throne, but was the eldest surviving legitimate male descendant of Charles IX). She managed to extract from the *råd* a reluctant agreement that he would be acknowledged as heir to the throne if she should die unmarried.

A year later, in 1650, the matter of the succession recurred. It was a year of social and economic unrest in Sweden. There had been a series of bad harvests, and there were great difficulties in paying off the soldiers no longer needed in Germany and returning them to civilian life. In addition, at a meeting of the *riksdag* the hard-pressed peasants demanded more strongly then ever that the crown should reclaim its alienated lands and revenues and that the nobility should be made to pay a fair share of the heavy burden of taxation.

1   We the undersigned Estates of the Realm [Clergy, Burghers and
    Peasants] . . . have cause to represent to Your Majesty, in all
    humility, that during these last years of war the crown has been
    greatly weakened by the alienation of its lands, and its interests
5   now require its lands to be restored to it in some convenient and
    proper fashion. For if this is not done we cannot see how Your
    Majesty can maintain your royal state and authority, or how the
    government of the country . . . can retain its present shape and
    constitution . . . for we esteem Your Majesty's royal power as the
10 buttress of our liberties, the one being bound up with the other
    . . . What have we gained beyond the seas if we lose our liberty at
    home?

Christina took advantage of the general discontent to get her own way over the succession. She led the nobles to believe that unless they agreed unconditionally to accept Charles as her heir and as hereditary ruler of Sweden she would side with the lower estates against them and order a 'Reduction' (the restoration to the crown of its alienated lands and revenues). The nobles would much have preferred to leave the succession question open. This would have allowed for a possible return at some future date to an elected monarchy with all its associated opportunities for aristocratic manipulation of the situation. Believing, however, that the queen was serious in her threats of a Reduction, they took fright and agreed to her demands in return for a supposed abandonment of the Reduction. On Christina's part it appears to have been a piece of sharp practice worthy of Gustav Vasa, for there is no evidence that she ever had any serious intention of ordering a Reduction. In fact, by the end of her reign in 1654 she had given away or sold almost all that remained of the crown lands.

* From an early age Christina had found the narrow intolerance of Swedish Lutheranism totally unsympathetic and by 1648 she had lost her faith. 'I no longer believed in the religion in which I was brought up', she wrote. Two years earlier, when she was already struggling with her spiritual crisis, she had been given a book written by the French philosopher Descartes, whose brand of liberal Roman Catholicism greatly impressed her. They began a lengthy correspondence and in 1649 she invited him to Stockholm. He was disappointed on his arrival by the rather offhand reception he received – Christina seems to have taken a dislike to him when they actually met – and was greatly distressed by the bitter weather. 'I think men's thoughts freeze here in winter, like the waters . . . I am not in my element here', he wrote. He survived the cold only a few months before dying of pneumonia; but his influence over Christina lived on after him.

In August 1651 Christina announced to the *råd* her intention to abdicate. Her official reasons for doing so were that it would be better for a man to rule the country for he could lead the army in war and that she herself wished to retire to the peace and quiet of private life. She added that there were other reasons which she could not mention. One of these must have been the fact that she had already secretly decided to become a Roman Catholic. This decision put her in a dilemma. Since 1617 catholicism had been illegal in Sweden. No catholics were permitted to live in the country, apart from a few foreigners with diplomatic privileges. In addition, Sweden's ruler was legally required by the constitution to be a professing Lutheran. She could not be both catholic and queen. Unaware of this religious difficulty facing Christina, the *råd*, through a united display of opposition engineered by Axel Oxenstierna who disliked Charles Gustavus and his family, managed to persuade her to remain as queen. The matter of abdication was left in abeyance for the time being.

For the next three years the unhappy woman threw herself into a hectic round of pleasure-seeking entertainment. Her court became the most brilliant, luxurious and extravagant, as well as the most coarse and immoral in Europe; government business was neglected, crown lands given away and state revenues squandered on festivities and favourites. In 1654 Christina, who had not given up the idea of abdicating, again informed the *råd* of her wishes in the matter, and indicated that this time her decision was irrevocable. Apart from the personal religious quandary in which she still found herself, she seems to have become seriously concerned for the Vasa succession in the light of her continued determination not to marry. If the accession of Charles Gustavus were delayed too long, the nobles might regret the decision made in his favour and, when the time finally arrived, simply elect someone else in his place. The only certain way to maintain the Vasa dynasty in power was to force the nobles' hands and ensure that Charles Gustavus became king as soon as possible.

The *riksdag* was accordingly summoned to meet at Uppsala in May 1654. The English ambassador was present at the meeting and described in detail the hall hung with tapestries, and the dais with the silver throne and the five crimson velvet chairs for the great officers of state surrounded by seats for the 500 or so members of the four estates. The queen made a short speech, praising Charles Gustavus's good qualities and hoping that the *riksdag* would 'consent to my resolution, since you may assure yourselves that none can dissuade me from my purpose'. There was a moving moment at the end when the leader of the peasants stepped forward and

1 Begged the queen to reconsider her decision to forsake her people. When he had ended his speech, he waddled up to the queen, took her by the hand and shook it heartily and kissed it two or three times; then turning his back on her, he pulled out of
5 his pocket a foul handkerchief and wiped the tears from his eyes.

The queen was not to be dissuaded even by such an emotional appeal and a few days later the formal abdication ceremony took place in the same great hall of the castle at Uppsala. The queen was divested of her royal robes and of the regalia, and the Abdication Document was read out. Christina curtsied to her successor, and left the room. She was no longer queen. Charles Gustavus immediately walked with his entourage to the nearby cathedral and was there crowned as Charles X. After attending a great state banquet that evening, Christina began the first stage of her journey into exile. When, a day or two later, she crossed the border into Denmark she is said to have jumped for joy, exclaiming 'Here I am at last at liberty and out of Sweden, where I hope never to return'. After being formally received into the Roman Catholic church, she eventually made her way to Rome where, despite the pension and the valuables which she brought out of Sweden, she died impoverished and largely forgotten, 35 years later.

  * Three months after the abdication, Axel Oxenstierna died. The last years of his life had not been particularly happy. The young queen, who liked to be the centre of attention, seems to have resented his authority. After she came of age in 1644 she ignored him more and more, disregarding his advice and undermining his position by favouring families known to be opposed to him. However, despite their differences she was not unaware of his worth. She called him 'a great minister of a great king', and after his death spoke of him as having been 'one of the outstanding men of the age'.

  For his part he found it difficult to come to terms with changed circumstances. As one nineteenth-century Swedish historian wrote of him, 'his political life terminated with the peace [of 1648]. It was the beginning of a new order of things, and in this, more than in the weakness of old age, lay his powerlessness'. His greatness lay in the past. As the trusted associate of Gustavus Adolphus and the architect of the Swedish collegiate system of government, Oxenstierna was assured of a prominent place in his country's history. His success in bringing Sweden out of the Thirty Years' War as a great power assured him an equally prominent place in European history.

Given his immense achievements at home and abroad, his great administrative and diplomatic gifts, why does Oxenstierna give the impression of a grey, rather negative personality at the end of 40 successful years in office? Probably because few historians, Swedes or non-Swedes, have wasted much time on him as an individual. Concerned with political or constitutional history, they have concentrated on his public persona, the cool and reserved junior partner and lonely successor of the ebullient Gustavus in whose shadow he stands. Calm and collected, introverted and intellectual, there is little evidence of the human touch in his public life. However, one historian believes that this is only because he:

1 Never found full outlet for his humane talents . . . In his personal outlook and interests [he was] a far more civilised and generous man than the king himself; selfless, devoted, kindly in his relations, capable of profound affection . . .

He was a man who served his monarch and his country with all his power, but from whom 'both they and the times exacted the wrong service', requiring from him a chief part in the organisation of 16 years of slaughter in Germany. This view of Oxenstierna as a tragic hero for whom the times were out of joint is an interesting one, but it is difficult to know whether it can be substantiated, for almost all the evidence available to English readers is to be found in necessarily impersonal official papers. However, there are one or two hints in a few personal letters and informal meetings which show him in a kindly light and as an affectionate family man. The English ambassador, who met him on a number of occasions in 1654, found him an entertaining conversationalist who told 'pleasant stories' of Gustavus Adolphus, and from whom he parted with genuine regret.

2 Charles X 1654–60

Charles was first and foremost a soldier and for much of his short reign Sweden was at war, first with Poland, and then with Muscovy, Denmark and Brandenburg. He did find time to marry a daughter of the Duke of Holstein-Gottorp in 1654 (see the map on page 86). This seemed an admirable match at the time, providing an ally for Sweden in the defence of Bremen-Verden against a possible Danish attack, but in the end it was to prove a political millstone (see page 86). To deal with the twin problems of social harmony (the need to placate the tax-paying peasantry) in 1655 and financial solvency (the need to fill the empty treasury) Charles managed to persuade the *riksdag* to agree to a limited Reduction of 'indispensable lands'. These were lands whose revenues were specifically allocated to the maintenance of the court, the armed forces and the mining industry. In addition, the nobility were to return a quarter of all lands received as gifts since 1632. The hope was that these measures would go some way to satisfying the demands of the lower estates and would produce enough money to solve the worst of the country's financial problems. Christina's extravagance had left the country close to bankruptcy. Unfortunately, the king died suddenly in 1660 before even this limited Reduction could be completed.

* Charles embarked on his foreign military adventures partly as a means of diverting attention away from problems at home, and partly because he enjoyed fighting and dreamed of emulating the achievements of his uncle, Gustavus Adolphus. In 1655 he attacked and overran western Poland, invaded Brandenburg and, temporarily, forced the elector to do homage to Sweden for East Prussia. In 1657 the Danes declared a war of revenge for the defeat of 1645. Charles immediately advanced on Denmark intending to seize the Sound. This would give Sweden control of Baltic trade with the west, especially the valuable and flourishing trade in 'naval stores' (timber, hemp, flax, tar and pitch) without which any maritime power was helpless. He invaded Jutland and then in January 1658, in an astonishing military exploit, he marched his army across the frozen waters of the Belts (see page 8) to Copenhagen. When he arrived at the gates of the city the Danes sued for peace. The treaty signed in February 1658 completed the destruction of Danish power begun by Oxenstierna in 1645. The southern provinces of Skåne, Blekinge and Halland were ceded to Sweden, together with the island of Bornholm. Sweden also acquired Bohuslän, greatly extending her direct access to the North Sea, and the port of Trondheim (see the map on page 9). In addition, Denmark renounced all anti-Swedish alliances and confirmed Sweden's exemption from the Sound dues.

Charles still hankered after control of the Sound as part of a larger scheme for a Swedish annexation of Denmark. In pursuit of this idea he launched a second and unprovoked attack on Denmark in July 1658. In September he gained temporary control of the Sound, but by doing so he earned the powerful enmity of the maritime powers (England and the Netherlands) who feared that Swedish control of the Sound would jeopardise the free passage of the vital naval stores. A large fleet was despatched to the Baltic to safeguard Dutch interests there, causing Charles considerable trouble. This, coupled with revolts in Skåne and Bornholm, left him in a weak position, but he was still full of plans for a winter attack on Norway when he died in February 1660 at the age of 38. A few months later the Pacification of the North ended Sweden's wars with Poland, Brandenburg, Denmark and Muscovy by a series of treaties. The long-standing dynastic feud between Sweden and Poland was brought to an end when the Polish Vasa kings agreed to give up their claim to the Swedish throne, Sweden was confirmed in her possession of Livonia, and Denmark recovered Trondheim and Bornholm.

* In 1660 Sweden had not achieved complete economic domination of the Baltic, nor did she control the Sound. Nevertheless, she was at the height of her imperial power. Possessing twice as much land overall as present day Sweden, she was one of the largest states in Europe, and possessed an enviable military reputation. Whether the acquisition of her scattered empire was in Sweden's long-term interest is a moot point (see chapter 6 for a discussion on this), but one historian at least believes that it was because of her new possessions that Sweden was able to expand into her modern borders on the Scandinavian peninsula by 1660. Without the use of those German bases she would not have been able to invade Denmark successfully and to win the land needed to consolidate her own territory along its natural frontiers. For the first time Sweden was a geographically unified country, well placed to defend herself against attack from outside. However, it was the enemy within which threatened her security during the long regency with which the next reign began.

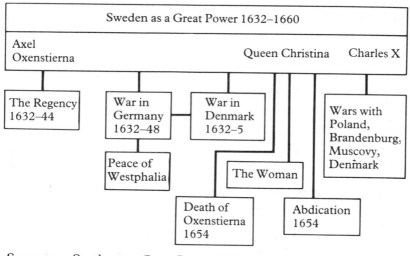

Summary – Sweden as a Great Power 1632–60

Making Notes on 'Sweden as a Great Power 1632–60'

This chapter is concerned with two main themes – the work of Oxenstierna after the death of Gustavus Adolphus in 1632, and Sweden's achievement of Great Power status by 1660. It would be helpful to write a few sentences in answer to the following questions:

1. Does the information in this chapter change your views on Oxenstierna?
2. How would you assess the importance of his work before 1632 compared with his work after that date?
3. Where do you consider that his greatness as a statesman lies?

4. Why can Sweden be said to have been just emerging as a Great Power in 1632 but certainly to have become one by 1660? Make a list of reasons for this change, arranging them in order of importance, and explain briefly why you have chosen that order.

(You will probably need to refer back to the previous chapter as well as using the information in this one to answer these questions.)

Answering essay questions on 'Sweden as a Great Power 1632–60'

The reigns of Christina and Charles X are unlikely to be the specific focus of an examinaton question, but they are sometimes included in a general question on the rise of Sweden to great power status in the mid-seventeenth century, such as:

1. 'How and when, in the seventeenth century, was Sweden at the height of her power?'
2. 'Describe and explain Sweden's territorial expansion during the reigns of Gustavus Adolphus, Christina and Charles X.'

You will find a discussion on how to answer general questions of this kind at the end of chapter 6.

However, specific questions are quite often set on the career of Axel Oxenstierna. These usually ask about the importance of a particular aspect of his work, and most often, though not always, cover the whole period of his chancellorship (1612–54). They may concentrate on his domestic achievements, for example:

3. 'Assess the importance of the part played by Axel Oxenstierna in Swedish domestic affairs between 1612 and 1632.'

Alternatively they may concentrate on his part in Sweden's rise to great power status:

4. 'Evaluate Axel Oxenstierna's contribution to the emergence of Sweden as a great power during the reigns of Gustavus Adolphus and Christina.'

Questions which begin 'Assess' or 'Evaluate' are asking for you to provide a reasoned judgement, based on information given in the course of your answer. In other words, to analyse your information. You are not being asked to write a narrative account of Oxenstierna's domestic achievements and to do so would earn few marks. You may find it helpful to simplify such questions by rephrasing them. Question 3, for example, could be reworded: 'How important was Oxenstierna's part in Swedish domestic affairs between 1612 and 1632?' The usual pattern for such answers is a two-part one along the lines of 'Yes, it was important/very important/most important because . . . but other contributions were also important because . . .' *or* 'No, it was not very important because . . . other contributions were equally/more important because . . .'. In planning your essay begin by drawing up a list of points for the contribution named in the question and a similar list for 'other contributions'. Make sure that the balance between the two parts of your essay (in this case, Oxenstierna v. others) is about half and half, and that the concluding paragraph sums up the views you have presented. As always with questions which contain dates, be careful to cover the whole period referred to, but not to overrun it.

Sometimes questions may be very wide-ranging indeed:

5. 'Does the death of Axel Oxenstierna bring an era of Swedish history to an end?'
6. 'Is the description of Axel Oxenstierna as 'the greatest statesman of his age' justified?'

To answer them well it is not enough to be able to write about Oxenstierna. You will need additional information which may well lie outside the period or region which you have studied. Question 5, for instance, pre-supposes a knowledge of events in Sweden after the death of Oxenstierna, while question 6 requires a knowledge of other statesmen with whom to compare him. Unless you are very sure of your ability to deal with questions of this sort, they are best avoided.

Source-based questions on 'Sweden as a Great Power 1632–60'

1 Christina and the Peasantry
Read the extract on page 76 and answer the following questions:
a) Explain the meaning of 'alienation' (line 4) and 'our liberties', as used in the petition on line 10. (4 marks)
b) Which estate was not a party to the petition? Why not? (4 marks)
c) What arguments are put forward by the petitioners in favour of royal action? (4 marks)
Now read the extract on page 78 and answer the following question:
d) What does this extract suggest about the relationship between crown and commonalty in 1654? Was it to be expected? Explain your answer. (8 marks)

2 Portraits

Carefully study the illustrations of Gustavus Adolphus (front cover), Gustav Vasa (page 15) and Axel Oxenstierna (page 43). Answer the following questions:

a) The portrait of Gustav Vasa was intended to create a particular impression. What was it? How did the artist achieve it? (4 marks)

b) From your knowledge of Gustav Vasa, is it likely that he would he have been pleased or not by this particular portrait? Explain your answer. (4 marks)

c) How far can a historian safely use the portraits of Gustavus Adolphus and Axel Oxenstierna as evidence of the sitters' personalities? (8 marks)

CHAPTER 5

Sweden in Decline 1660–1721

With the death of Charles X the second, expansionist, period of Vasa rule came to an end and the third and final phase, that of decline, began. The 61 years from 1660 (the accession of Charles XI as a child of four) to 1721 (the end of the Great Northern War) saw two significant developments in Swedish history – the rise and fall of absolutism, and the collapse of the empire.

1 Charles XI and Absolutism

a) The Long Regency 1660–72

The first few years of the regency were uneventful, but after that the situation deteriorated. Financial difficulties and social discontent increased as the result of poor government, for the regents (the chief officers of state, who were all members of the *råd*) formed an oligarchy largely animated by self-interest. At their head was the attractive and cultured but lazy, indecisive and irresponsible Magnus de la Gardie, the chancellor.

Among the most pressing difficulties which faced the regents was the question of the army. It quickly became clear to them that Sweden was too poor to maintain a standing army large enough to protect her sprawling empire in peace time without the help of foreign subsidies. As a subsidy-hunter Sweden soon found herself in a position of weakness, dependent on foreign paymasters, and slipping from her place as a Great Power. The regents mistakenly believed that the promise of Sweden's neutrality was sufficient recompense for their paymasters, and failed to realise that sooner or later more was going to be asked of them. It therefore came as a nasty shock when in 1674 France demanded that a Swedish army, which French subsidies had equipped, should be sent to Germany before any more money was paid over. The regents had no choice but to concur if they were to avoid major financial problems, and in a very short time Sweden found herself involved in a war against Brandenburg, the Netherlands and Denmark from which de la Gardie, who was universally blamed for the whole affair, struggled vainly to extricate her.

In the course of what came to be called the Scanian War, Sweden was defeated in Germany and came close to disaster on the Scandinavian peninsula as well. In 1675 the Swedish army was defeated by a numerically inferior Brandenburg army. News of this defeat encouraged Denmark to imprison the Duke of Holstein-Gottorp, who had promised military assistance to the Swedes, and he was forced to surrender his castles to Denmark. This was a serious blow to Sweden for the alliance with Holstein-Gottorp, initiated by the marriage first of Charles IX and then of Charles X into the ducal family, was a corner-stone of Swedish foreign policy. The duke's strategically placed but scattered lands lay partly within the Holy Roman Empire and partly in Schleswig in southern Denmark (see the map below). The Holstein-Gottorp connection not only assured Sweden of a backdoor entry into Denmark, but also acted as 'a stopper for the Jute', preventing any Danish surprise attack to the south. Danish control of Holstein-Gottorp left Sweden's German possessions vulnerable.

The Swedish fleet, like the army, suffered a serious defeat. The naval commanders had no experience of warfare and the ships were too old and too few in number. As a result, a combined Danish-Dutch fleet gained control of the Baltic. Charles XI, who had been declared of age in 1702 provided the only bright spot in the war. He saved the province of Halland from the Danes and, by his reckless bravery at the head of the army, defeated them in Skåne at the battle of Lund in 1676. By his efforts he saved Sweden from complete disaster. (This unexpected military success created in him a passion for the army which characterised the rest of his reign.) However, he could not save Sweden's possessions in Germany – in November 1678 the last of them was lost. As it turned out, the loss was only temporary, for France needed a

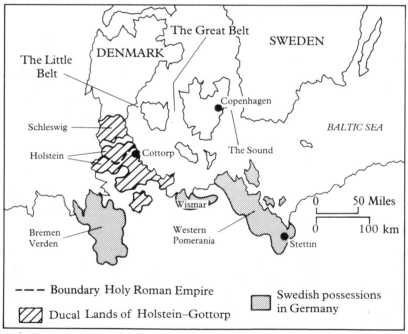

Sweden and Holstein–Gottorp

strong ally in northern Europe and was unwilling to see Sweden seriously weakened. As a result, in 1679 the French imposed a peace settlement on all the combatants, which restored the pre-war territorial status quo, but the war had revealed the incipient weakness of Sweden's scattered empire and had left her military reputation in tatters.

The damage done to national pride by the war had an important effect on Swedish government policy during the remainder of the reign. It determined Charles on two things – to find a way to pay and equip the army without foreign subsidies, and to keep Sweden out of foreign wars.

b) Charles XI 1660–97

Charles Xl was not a preposessing figure. He was parsimonious and shabbily dressed, quick-tempered, obstinate and narrow minded, and was not noticeably intelligent or imaginative. His general education had been neglected by the regency government and his academic achievements were greatly hampered by what appears to have been severe dyslexia. His main interests were hunting and military exercises. However, on the credit side, he was courageous and hardworking, sincere in his religion and with a strong sense of duty to his country. Although he had none of the Vasa facility with words, he had inherited to the full their knack of getting on with ordinary people and, as 'King Greycloak', appears as the hero of many a local legend.

i) The Growth of Absolutism

In 1675 a commission had been set up by the *riksdag* on the order of the king to investigate alleged irregularities in the conduct of the former regents. Its findings confirmed that there had been mismanagement and financial malpractice, and in 1680 a meeting of the *riksdag* was called to consider what should be done. It was decided that the ex-regents should be made to refund the enormous sums of money which the treasury had lost through their maladministration or which they had appropriated to their own use. This was a terrible blow to them, but worse was to follow. The lesser nobility had for some years felt growing resentment at what they considered to be the excessive privileges enjoyed by the members of the *råd* and the rest of the higher aristocracy. They therefore joined with the three non-noble estates at the same meeting of the *riksdag* to formulate a reply to some very leading questions put to them by the king regarding his constitutional position. They assured Charles that he was not *obliged* to consult the *råd* in matters of government, that he was free to make decisions in accordance with his own 'good and just judgement', and that, under the law, he was responsible for his actions only to God. In view of the empty treasury, and the fear that liability for tax might be extended from the peasantry to other estates in order to meet the shortfall, the *riksdag* also asked that a major Reduction (resumption of alienated crown lands) should be begun.

In 1682 Charles was given full control over the Reduction. All alienated lands in the conquered territories were quickly reclaimed and any future alienation of lands there was forbidden. During the next few years nearly 80 per cent of all alienated lands were resumed (see the Table of Changes in Landownership on page 18). The resumptions bore most heavily on the higher aristocracy which had benefited most from alienation. Their economic power was greatly weakened and that of the crown was greatly increased. Swedish literature is full of little 'prayers' expressing the bitterness of the nobility on this issue:

> 1 Blessed be the memory of the great royal economist Charles XI,
>   who took five manors from my grandfather. May God not admit
>   him among the ranks of the blessed on the Last Day for we would
>   be given homespun instead of the snow-white garments which are
> 5 our due . . . he would make the Almighty Himself cast about for
>   means of retrenchment . . .

It is true that on some occasions the Reduction was pursued with great rigour against 'innocent heirs, unlucky spouses and unwitting purchasers' of alienated land. So much so, that 'often the crown's rights meant the subject's wrongs'. As a contemporary nobleman complained:

> 1 All depended upon the king's grace, and no subject was to have
>   such a title [to his land] that the king was not able to deprive him
>   of it with some show of legality and give it away to whoever he
>   chose.

The great magnates claimed to be financially ruined, and some were – Magnus de la Gardie, whose income had been equal to one twentieth of the revenues of the crown in 1679, was reduced to living on royal bounty ten years later – but now there was plenty of money in the royal treasury, and there was no need for the king to seek foreign subsidies to maintain the army. The king was able once again to 'live of his own', as Gustav Vasa had done. This fact had a direct bearing on a further concession by the *riksdag*, when later, in 1689, they compromised the right to grant or withold taxes, a privilege which they might have been expected to preserve as their last hold over the king and his government; however, they did not see it like that. Since the crisis of 1650 the estates had been concerned, not with using the crown's financial embarrassments to obtain control over state expenditure, but with forcing a Reduction so that the king would 'live of his own' and would not require the granting of taxes at all. As long as the Reduction was concluded to their satisfaction, they were not interested in asserting constitutional rights over finance.

In 1682, in a follow-up to the *riksdag*'s decision in 1680, the status of the *råd* was further reduced when its name was changed from the State Council to the King's Council. From being a council of nobles by whose advice the king governed, it had become a council whose members were merely the king's ministers, doing his bidding. In the same year the *riksdag* proceeded further along the road to the establishment of absolutism. Free speech within the *riksdag* was threatened after the king objected to the remarks of one member on a matter of law and demanded that the remarks be withdrawn on the grounds that only he could decide the law; for a member of the *riksdag* to do so was to infringe the royal prerogative. The *riksdag* immediately and subserviently agreed that it was:

1 Quite absurd to force Your Majesty to take opinion of your estates
  whenever you wish to make any statute, regulation, proclamation
  or ordinance. Should the king find anything in the Law of
  Sweden which it may be necessary to alter or clarify or improve
5 then it is accepted that the king has the right and power to do it.

They asked – 'without any presumption or trenching on Your Majesy's rights and prerogative' – that the king's wishes in such cases should be transmitted to the *riksdag*; but only for information, and not for discussion, they hastened to assure him. When the king took them at their word, and tested their reaction by promulgating an Ecclesiastical Law without consulting them first, they made no objection, although it resulted in a considerable extension of royal control over the church.

The *riksdag*, whose members had become ever more fawning, then went on to pass an incredible piece of legislation. They imposed retrospective censorship on all their documents since 1633 which might in any way be considered to reflect on the king's prerogative:

1 From the humble duty and obligation which binds us until death
  to our most gracious . . . good and imcomparable king and master
  . . . we derive a deep loathing for all such insubordinate speeches
  and discourses and from our hearts wish they had never been
5 thought or uttered . . . we order that all such offensive passages in
  the Minutes be abolished and annihilated . . .

In 1693 came the final accolade. Charles XI, they resolved:

1 Is by God, Nature and the Crown's high hereditary right . . . an
  absolute sovereign king, whose commands are binding upon all,
  and who is responsible to no one on earth for his actions, but has
  power and might at his pleasure, as a Christian king, to rule and
5 govern his kingdom.

They could go no further. No wonder that a year later an English visitor to Sweden believed that:

1 So favourable had been the Conjuncture for the Advancement of the King's Authority that he scarce needed to ask whatever he desired: each of the Estates striving which could outbid the other in their Concessions . . . These Dispositions of the People . . .
5 gave him an opportunity to lay the Foundations of as Absolute a Sovereignty as any Prince in Europe possesses.

The collaboration of crown and nobility in the 'aristocratic constitutionalism' based on the power of the *råd* and instituted by the Accession Charter of Gustavus Adolphus in 1612, had made way for royal absolutism and the exercise of divine right. Why had the change been made so easy for the king and been so peacefully carried out? He had not needed to use any violence to achieve it, for there had been no opposition. Absolutism had been established constitutionally by the *riksdag*, who created it entirely peacefully over a period of 13 years. Their decisions were accepted, if not actively supported by the majority of the population who, after the troubles of the regency years, were prepared to surrender political freedom in the hope of obtaining good government.

After the discrediting of the ex-regents, divisions between the estates allowed the king to exploit the situation to his own advantage. The loss of influence by the *råd*, and the success of the Reduction left the aristocracy politically isolated and economically weak. Power passed unchallenged to the crown – there was no one able or willing to oppose the king successfully – and the *riksdag's* declarations of 1693 were inevitable. However, historians are divided about how far Charles planned his manipulation of the *riksdag*. There is not enough evidence available on which to make a firm decision, but it seems likely that, meeting no resistance, he simply continued to push forward until he could go no further. His 'quiet revolution' marked the defeat not just of a political theory but of an unpopular social class, whose undoing was completed by the introduction of a Table of Ranks. This laid down that all posts in civil and military government service should in future be filled according to merit rather than according to birth. The growth of an efficient bureaucracy closely dependent upon the sovereign for its appointment and pay was one of the permanent legacies of the reign.

ii) The Army
With the land and revenues available to him from the Reduction, Charles XI solved the problem of how to maintain an army in peace-time without the aid of foreign subsidies. He introduced an improved version of Gustavus Adolphus's system of army maintenance, known as the allotment system. This involved the settling of the native

conscript army upon the land. Each soldier was assigned to work on a farm when he was not on training manoeuvres. As his pay he received either the produce of the farm, or the whole or part of the taxes or rent (usually paid in kind) due to the crown from that farm. While a small mercenary force had to be employed to protect Swedish possessions overseas, the army at home thus became self-supporting. In addition, as all the men from one unit were allocated to farms in the area from which the unit was recruited, mobilisation was quick and easy, especially as all details were meticulously planned in advance under the personal supervision of the king.

As a result, Charles bequeathed to his son a well-trained and well-equipped native army numbering perhaps as many as 90,000 men. However, it had one inbuilt disadvantage. The system of payment in kind would not work well if the army had to fight abroad. But as Charles XI had no intention of fighting anywhere at all if he could help it, it was not for him a problem.

Neither did the navy escape his attention. A new naval base, named Karlskrona after himself, was begun in southern Sweden in 1680. Better placed in relation to the Swedish overseas empire, and frozen for a shorter time in winter than the old naval base in Stockholm harbour, it quickly developed into an important operational centre. The fleet itself was reorganised and enlarged into an up-to-date fighting force of 43 ships so that at the end of the reign Sweden was well protected on the sea as well as on land.

iii) Foreign Affairs 1679–97
The end of the Scanian War in 1679 ushered in a new era of peaceful cooperation between Sweden and Denmark, celebrated in 1680 by the marriage of Charles to Ulrica Eleanor, sister of the Danish king. However, despite Charles's wish for good relations with his neighbour, the two countries were soon on bad terms again. The trouble arose over Holstein-Gottorp, whose duke had been freed and restored to his possessions in 1679 at the end of the Scanian War. Both Sweden and Denmark considered that control of the duke and his lands was essential to their own well-being and, when Denmark invaded Holstein-Gottorp in 1683 and incorporated the duke's Schleswig lands into the kingdom of Denmark, a full-scale Scandinavian war seemed likely to follow. The danger was averted and a peace treaty was signed in 1689 by which Denmark agreed to restore the duke's lands once again and to confirm his independence. However, the issue remained a sensitive one and trouble was to flare up again at the beginning of the next reign.

2 Charles XII 1697–1718

In 1697, at the age of 15, Charles XII became absolute king of Sweden. He was soon faced with a formidable anti-Swedish coalition which led to the start of the Great Northern War in 1700. It was still in progress when he was killed in 1718 at the age of 36.

a) The Coalition against Sweden

The problem of Holstein-Gottorp surfaced again immediately on the death of Charles XI when Danish troops briefly entered ducal territory. Charles XII at once showed his support for the duke, who was not only made commander-in-chief of the Swedish forces in Germany, but also married Charles's elder sister. It was not lost on the Danes that this could have important implications for the Swedish succession if Charles should die without issue. The situation between the two countries again deteriorated, but while Sweden was making preparations for a probable war against her old enemy and neighbour, unknown to her government a much more serious challenge was being prepared.

Denmark was negotiating energetically to build up a coalition against Sweden. It involved the elector of Saxony, who after 1697 was also Augustus II, king of Poland, whose ambitions included a plan to regain Livonia (once Polish) and its great port of Riga from the Swedes. In 1699 the tsar, Peter I, joined the coalition in the hopes that by recovering former Muscovite possessions in Ingria and along the River Neva he could provide himself with a 'window on the west' and direct access to the Baltic. He had met Augustus in Poland the previous summer and they had signed a treaty for joint action against Sweden, in anticipation of an easy victory against the young and untried Charles XII. Charles, however, was to prove himself a brilliant tactician and an outstanding commander. An experienced French officer who served in the Swedish army wrote a first hand account of Swedish drill and of Charles's skill in military manoeuvres, which leaves the king's military ability in no doubt. He was indeed the 'Terror of the North' – at least until 1708.

By the autumn of 1699 Denmark, Poland and Muscovy had completed their preparations and in February 1700 the war began.

b) The Great Northern War 1700–21

The Swedes were expecting an attack from Denmark but were taken by surprise when the war began on two fronts at once. The Danish attack was concentrated on the Holstein-Gottorp lands in the west, while in the east Augustus swept into Livonia and Peter advanced on Ingria and Estonia. To ensure freedom of trade through the Baltic, both Britain and Holland wanted to preserve the balance of power there. This would be endangered if Denmark obtained total control of the Sound by defeating Sweden. An Anglo-Dutch fleet therefore came to Sweden's aid by providing extra transport for the movement of Charles's army to the Danish island of Zealand. From there he was able to threaten

'The Crossing of the Dvina' by Stawert, 1701

Copenhagen, the Danish capital. In August 1700 Denmark withdrew from the war, having agreed once more to recognise the independence of the Duke of Holstein-Gottorp and to restore his lands.

Charles and his troops then left Denmark for the Livonian port of Pernau. From there they made a forced-march through mud and slush into Ingria, where they took Peter by suprise as he was besieging the fortress of Narva. With only 8,000 men Charles heavily defeated a Muscovite army of 23,000 in a November snowstorm, forcing Peter to withdraw from Ingria. Charles also left Ingria, and marched south to winter in Livonia. In June 1701, after receiving reinforcements which brought his army up to 18,000 men, he crossed the river Dvina under fierce enemy artillery fire. After destroying a combined Russo-Saxon army nearly twice the size of his own near Riga, he went on to occupy Courland.

There is some evidence that Charles thought of invading Russia at this point, but that he changed his mind in favour of an attack on Poland. Success there could end the dynastic union of Saxony and Poland and turn Poland, with its valuable grain port of Danzig, into a Swedish client state. In 1702 he marched his army, largely unopposed, straight through Poland from north to south, capturing Wilno, Warsaw, and Cracow as he went. In one of the few set battles of the

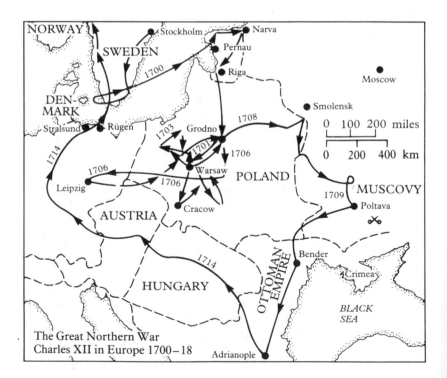

The Great Northern War
Charles XII in Europe 1700–18

campaign, Charles's brother-in-law, the Duke of Holstein-Gottorp was killed. For the next three years Augustus and Charles chivied each other ineffectually round Poland, which was itself in the throes of a civil war. In 1704 Charles managed to depose Augustus and to replace him with a Swedish puppet as king of Poland. Two years later Charles had driven all Augustus's troops out of Poland and had invaded Saxony where he remained for the next twelve months.

This time was spent preparing for a campaign against Peter, raising money and making plans to deal with the reorganised and re-equipped Muscovite army which had reappeared in the Baltic provinces while Charles had been chasing Augustus round Poland and into Saxony. During those years Peter had invaded Courland and had laid waste large areas of Estonia and Livonia. The whole of Ingria was again in his hands and the foundations had been laid for his new city of St. Petersburg at the mouth of the Neva. Charles's Baltic empire was crumbling to pieces, while the tsar's Baltic empire was just beginning to take shape. Nevertheless, faced with the prospect of a Swedish invasion, the tsar made overtures for peace throughout 1706. Provided he could keep his new city of St. Petersburg on the Neva, he was willing to surrender all his other Baltic conquests. The war might have been brought to an early end, but for Charles's determination to expel Peter's troops by force of arms from the Baltic states, and from Poland where they were supporting Augustus's efforts to recover his throne and threatening the safety of the Swedish puppet king.

i) Charles in Muscovy
In the spring of 1708 Charles marched east with more than 40,000 men. His plans were on a grand scale. He intended to go with his main army by the northern road to Smolensk and then directly to Moscow, where he would demand Peter's unconditional surrender and bring the war to an end with a dictated peace. The remainder of the army would be divided into three sections. One would invade Ingria from Finland and capture St. Petersburg, another would march from Poland into the Ukraine to support the Cossack rising against the tsar which was being organised there, and the third section, under the command of General Lewenhaupt, would march from Riga with a large baggage and supply train to join Charles on the road to Moscow.

Unfortunately, Charles had grossly underestimated the difficulties he would face. He did not know the terrain, he had not allowed for the problems of supply or of maintaining morale so far from home and, above all, he had no control over the atrocious weather. As he advanced, the enemy army retreated before him, laying waste the countryside through which he would have to pass. The Muscovites were eventually brought to stand and fight in what was to be Charles's last successful pitched battle. It took place on the banks of the Dnieper in June and secured the river crossing for him. He decided to wait there for a while for Lewenhaupt and the baggage train to arrive. He waited in vain. Losing patience, he moved on towards Smolensk, but Peter's scorched earth policy resulted in 'murmurings of the soldiery' about the shortage of bread and he was soon forced to turn south in search of food. Lewenhaupt meanwhile had been making only slow progress and was still far behind when in September he was set upon by a Muscovite army. The baggage train was captured and half his men were killed. There would be few reinforcements and no supplies now for Charles.

The Swedes were in despair when the news arrived. They were exhausted by long marches through inhospitable forests and were near starvation, for when they had at last arrived at their new destination they found that the area had already been ravaged. Peter's soldiers had got there first. There was nothing for it but to move on again. Charles, joined now by the survivors from Lewenhaupt's army, decided to postpone his attack on Moscow until the following year. Instead he marched his demoralised troops towards the Ukraine. He was confident that once he made contact with the leader of the Don Cossacks, Ivan Mazeppa, supplies of all kinds would be immediately forthcoming. Even the news that the Swedish army sent to reconquer Ingria had totally failed in its mission did not discourage him.

Mazeppa, who wanted independence from Muscovy for the Cossacks, had offered Charles military assistance against Peter, but when the Swedes arrived they found that the Muscovite army had already sacked the Cossack capital and that Mazeppa was now a fugitive. Disappointingly, therefore, he could provide little help in the way of men or materials for the Swedes, but at least supplies of food were available. Charles established winter quarters and settled down to wait for the arrival of the Swedish army from Poland. The winter of 1708–9 turned out to be the worst in living memory. In the Ukraine the cold was appalling. His army was encamped on the open steppe in weather so bitter that, it was said, even the birds froze to death in mid-flight. One Swedish soldier described in his diary how:

1 On Christmas Eve and the day before the cold was so intense the whole road was littered with men and horses who had been frozen to death, and with abandoned baggage and hospital waggons, so that it was pitiful to behold. There wasn't a regiment in which
5 some of the officers and many of the men were not injured or killed [by the cold] and most of the drivers perished.

So many Swedish soldiers died of cold, or suffered severe frostbite that by the New Year only about 24,000 were left. A thaw brought floods and made communications impossible. In addition, there was no sign of the reinforcements from Poland – in fact, they had never set out – and no prospect of any other aid, apart from that offered by another group of Cossacks, who were soon crushed by the tsar's soldiers. Supplies were again running low and numbers were dwindling daily from cold and disease when Charles began preparations for a summer campaign to draw Peter into battle before the Swedish situation deteriorated further. On 1 May 1709 he laid siege to the fortress of Poltava to the east of Kiev with about 20,000 troops, and there, two months later, he was defeated by an army twice the size of his own. Even before the battle began, disaster had struck the Swedes. Charles had been seriously wounded in the foot during a preliminary skirmish a few days earlier. He was brought by litter to the battlefield, where he was at one time in some danger of capture. The generals, including Lewenhaupt, deputed to act for him did not see entirely eye to eye with one another, and an attempt at a surprise attack under cover of darkness failed. Catastrophe followed. In the muddle of conflicting orders, a third of the Swedish infantry was destroyed before reaching the battlefield. Most of the remainder perished when they arrived there. Swedish losses were very heavy – 10,000 killed or captured, and large numbers wounded. The survivors, mainly cavalry, began the long retreat towards the Dnieper.

When they reached the river, Charles and Mazeppa were persuaded to leave the rest of the army and to make good their escape. After crossing the river with a small number of followers they fled through Poland. From there they crossed the border into the Ottoman Empire, where they were received by the sultan with some surprise and little pleasure. Charles was to remain there for the next five years.

The rest of the army, for whom there were not enough boats to cross the river, had been put under the command of Lewenhaupt by Charles. They were to march southeastwards towards the Crimea, where they would rejoin the king. Lewenhaupt, who was by now in poor health, seems to have had a hard time keeping the men under control and to have been doubtful of their willingness to fight if called upon to do so. When they were approached by Muscovite cavalry he panicked. Apparently, believing the enemy contingent to be much larger than it was, he simply surrendered. Charles's army had ceased to exist.

Poltava was not only a turning point in the war, but it also tipped the balance of power in eastern Europe in favour of Russia for the first time. Russian troops quickly consolidated their hold on the Baltic provinces. They overran the Karelian isthmus, and captured the fortress of Viborg. Riga capitulated to them, and the remaining Swedish possessions of Reval, Pernau and Kexholm were captured in 1710. In the same year Peter married his niece to the Duke of Courland and, when the latter died only two months later, he sent troops to garrison the duchy on behalf of the widow. The Swedish puppet king was driven out of Poland and Augustus was restored to his throne. Swedish influence in Poland was at an end, whilst Russian influence there had begun. On the Scandinavian peninsula itself, Denmark took advantage of Charles's defeat and flight to the Ottoman Empire to re-enter the war and to attack southern Sweden; however, the affair was not well managed and it ended in defeat for the Danes.

ii) Charles in the Ottoman Empire

It was with some reluctance that the sultan granted asylum to Charles and his ally, Mazeppa. The tsar demanded Charles's expulsion from the empire but the sultan refused. Peter offered a few minor diplomatic concessions and the sultan agreed to send Charles back to Sweden if he was given a safe conduct by the tsar and was accompanied by an Ottoman military escort. Charles refused to go. The tsar sent an ultimatum insisting on immediate departure. On the day the ultimatum arrived in December 1710, the sultan declared war on Muscovy, less out of concern for Charles than to signify opposition to Muscovy's interference in Ottoman affairs. This meant that for the time being Charles could not be sent home, but must remain in the Ottoman Empire where he was proving himself a somewhat troublesome guest. He had rapidly become the centre of a series of complicated political intrigues, plots and counter-plots directed against Peter and involving the khan of the Crimea (a vassal of the sultan). Charles long continued to hope that the sultan could be persuaded to join him and the khan in a concerted attack on Peter from several directions at once.

Charles's ultimate intention was for 50,000 Ottoman soldiers to march into Poland and to join up with a new Swedish army to be based in Pomerania. He sent urgent communications to Stockholm, pressing the government there to raise the necessary money, men and materials for the new army and on no account to consider making peace with Muscovy. These orders put the Swedish government in a difficult position, for they had accepted the so-called Neutrality Conventions drawn up by the Emperor and the maritime powers, which laid down that Sweden's German possessions should neither be invaded by foreigners nor used by the Swedes as bases from which to launch an attack. Charles repudiated the Conventions on the grounds that, relying on God's help and the justice of his cause, he was entitled to employ all resources open to him to defeat his enemies – including the use of Swedish Pomerania as a base for his army. With great difficulty, in 1712 the Swedish government managed to find the money to meet Charles's demands. They raised and equipped an army of 9000 men which successfully crossed the Baltic to Rügen in Pomerania. However, its supply ships were captured by the Danes and without supplies the army could not hope to survive for long. Although it was unexpectedly successful in an initial encounter with the Danes, in 1713 it was forced to surrender to them. So the last Swedish military expedition to Germany ended in ignominy.

Meanwhile, the sultan was occupied with his own campaign against the tsar, and in July 1711 the Ottomans surrounded and totally defeated Peter's army on the banks of the Pruth river in the Balkans. The terms of the peace treaty which the Ottomans agreed with Peter were generous. In Charles's opinion they were criminally so, for he clung misguidedly to the belief that the war was being fought primarily for his benefit. Peter had informed his negotiating envoys that to satisfy the Ottomans he was prepared if necessary to surrender all his Baltic conquests (except Ingria), and to recognise Charles's puppet as rightful king of Poland. But the Ottomans were content with much less, and, despite a frenzied dash to the scene by Charles, the sultan's officials agreed a settlement in which Sweden gained nothing.

Further war between Peter and the sultan and a serious outbreak of plague which spread across eastern Europe combined to keep Charles in the Ottoman Empire. However, in 1713 Peter and the sultan were at peace, and the plague had abated. There now seemed nothing to delay Charles's departure further and he was ordered by the sultan to leave. But Charles would not agree to go. He claimed to have evidence of a plot by, among others, the tsar and the now restored Augustus to kidnap him, despite his safe conduct, as he travelled through Poland. There followed the so-called *kalabalik* – a tumult or affray – when Charles barricaded himself into his house and refused to come out. He defended it for 8 hours with the help of some 40 followers against an Ottoman army of, it is said, 12,000 men with artillery, and was only captured when he fell to the ground after getting himself tangled up with his spurs. He was seized and eventually taken in semi-captivity to the small Balkan town of Demotika. Shortly after his arrival there, he took to his bed, where he remained for the next ten months.

When the War of the Spanish Succession, which had been going on in western Europe since 1702, finally came to an end in March 1714, the way was clear for Charles to return home through the Holy Roman Empire, instead of having to go through Poland. At the end of October 1714 Charles finally left the Ottoman Empire. He covered nearly 900 miles, the majority of it on horseback, in only 13 days. He arrived exhausted in the middle of the night of 10–11 November at the besieged fortress of Stralsund in Pomerania and, instead of proceeding speedily to Sweden to take control there, he remained to conduct a year-long defence of Stralsund. One of his first actions was to issue a Privateer Ordinance whose aim was to extend the activities and number of Swedish privateers already harassing shipping in the Baltic. This angered the maritime powers, who were still concerned about their supplies of naval stores. Their response was to second a detachment of the British fleet to the Danes who, with this reinforcement, were able to prevent Swedish help reaching Stralsund. The fortress fell in December 1715 and Charles, who had escaped two or three days earlier, at last returned home to Sweden, which had struggled with bad harvests, a severe outbreak of plague, economic difficulties and foreign invasions, but had managed somehow to survive 15 years of war and the absence of her king.

iii) Charles Back in Sweden

While Charles was still lingering in the Ottoman Empire or occupied in defending Stralsund, matters had gone from bad to worse for Sweden and her colonies. Between 1712 and 1715 her German provinces went the way of the Baltic ones. From 1711 onwards, Saxon and Muscovite troops joined with Danish forces in attacks on Holstein-Gottorp, which was occupied by Denmark in 1713, and on Pomerania, part of which was occupied in the same year by a combined force. In 1712 the Danes seized Bremen. This encouraged Hanover and Prussia to intervene. Hanover occupied Verden, in order to 'safeguard' it for Sweden, and in 1715 obtained Bremen from the Danes. By the end of that year both the king of Prussia, who had already occupied Stettin, and the elector of Hanover had formally declared war on Sweden. At the beginning of 1716, with the loss of Wismar to a combined Danish-Prussian-Hanoverian force, Sweden's lands outside the Scandinavian peninsula had all gone. Even on the peninsula itself there were losses, for Peter had occupied a large part of Finland by the end of 1714.

Not discouraged by the near hopeless situation which he found on his return to Sweden, Charles began gathering men and materials for yet another campaign, this time against Danish Norway. In March 1716 he occupied the Norwegian capital without difficulty, but was forced to return home by the news that Skåne, one of Sweden's southern provinces, was threatened with a joint invasion by Muscovy and Denmark, in alliance with Hanover and assisted by Britain. However, because of quarrels among the allies, the invasion came to nothing, while widespread diplomatic activity brought the war no nearer to an end. Therefore, in the autumn of 1718 Charles again set out on an expedition to Norway. On 30 November he was killed while besieging Fredrikshald. He had been shot through the head.

iv) The End of the War

Charles's death did not bring the war to an immediate end. Peter continued to harass the Swedish coast around Stockholm and to do considerable damage inland, in an attempt to bring the Swedes 'to see reason' and make peace with Muscovy. However, the Swedes were not prepared to do so and instead, in 1719, made an agreement with Hanover, by which Bremen-Verden were ceded to the elector in return for financial and naval assistance from Britain, of which the elector was also king. Early in 1720 Sweden ceded the port of Stettin and part of Pomerania to Prussia, again in return for financial assistance. Sweden managed to keep the rest of Pomerania including Stralsund, and Wismar in Mecklenburg, as the sole surviving remnants of her German possessions. A treaty with Denmark, also made in 1720, returned to Sweden all Danish conquests and allowed Sweden to keep her gains in Norway. Denmark further undertook not to assist the tsar against Sweden. In return Sweden gave up her long standing exemption from the Sound dues and agreed not to give aid to the Duke of Holstein-Gottorp to recover his lands in Schleswig, which Denmark kept.

Peace having been effected between the two Scandinavian powers, Sweden looked forward confidently to recovering her Baltic provinces from the tsar with the promised assistance of the British navy. She was disappointed. The fleet remained inactive, for Britain had become anxious to see peace in the north. Sweden had no choice but to obtain what terms she could from Muscovy. In August 1721, the treaty of Nystad was signed. Sweden ceded Livonia, Estonia, Ingria and part of Karelia to Muscovy – all the coastline from Riga to Viborg was lost. In return, Sweden recovered Finland, and secured a promise of non-interference by the tsar in Swedish internal affairs and an agreement enabling her to import duty-free grain from Riga.

* It was a bitter day for Sweden when, at the peace celebrations in St. Petersburg, the tsar was proclaimed 'Father of the Fatherland, Peter the Great, Emperor of all Russia'. The Great Northern War had changed the balance of power in the region out of all recognition. In 1700 the rise of Russia could no more have been predicted than could the fall of Sweden. But by 1721 Russia had defeated Sweden, conquered the Baltic provinces, with their vital access to the sea, and expanded Russian influence into Poland and north Germany, while Sweden would never again be a great power, never again be all supreme in the Baltic. Shorn of her overseas possessions, she withdrew into the Scandinavian peninsula, no longer a European power – merely a Baltic one. It was cold comfort that she was stronger territorially, by virtue of the Scanian provinces and the Norwegian lands, than she had been in 1611 before the imperial adventure began. The only consolation was that Denmark had failed to recover control of both sides of the Sound and was not herself strong enough to make a bid for Baltic supremacy. The war had left a very even balance of power between the two Scandinavian countries. If nothing else came out of the war to Sweden's advantage, it ended old conflicts and brought a prospect of peace with her neighbour for the foreseeable future.

c) Domestic Affairs

Charles XII is so closely identified with the 'warrior king' image and with the Great Northern War that other aspects of his reign are too often ignored.

i) Early Years of the Reign
When he succeeded to the throne in April 1697 a regency council of six members, presided over by the queen-grandmother, took control in accordance with his father's will. Remembering the troubles which beset the previous regency council in 1676, when its members were called to account by Charles XI and found wanting, the newly-appointed regents were none too willing to continue in office any longer than was absolutely necessary. Nor was the rest of Sweden anxious to

risk years of regency misgovernment again. The one and only full *riksdag* of the reign met in November 1697 and, although Charles XII was only 15-years-old, a deputation from all four estates petitioned that he should 'govern for himself'. He accepted, and a few days later the government was formally handed over to him. He had become absolute ruler of Sweden.

In the following three years Charles learnt much about administration and the judicial process, the art of diplomacy and the exercise of military command. In 1700 he exchanged a theoretical study of tactics and strategy for the realities of war, and it was war which remained his chief concern for the rest of his life. But during what he called his 'lazy dog-days' in the Ottoman Empire and in the years after his return to Sweden, he developed a hitherto latent interest in domestic reform.

ii) Domestic Reforms

Charles XII in the guise of a domestic reformer might seem surprising, but the signs that he was something more than a soldier were there from the beginning of the reign. Judicial and other government records of that time show him to have been concerned for social justice and for the rights as well as the duties of the individual, and, in line with his rationalist outlook, as having an interest in scientific developments. He was certainly not the 'illiterate' described by some nineteenth-century Swedish historians for, under the influence of the architect and designer Tessin, Charles as a young man became deeply involved in the theatre, in art and architecture and in the study of French literature. He continued to correspond with Tessin, under whose guidance he embarked on the study of antiquities and of music during his Ottoman Empire period of inactivity. It was then, too, that he supervised the production of an illustrated book on Swedish drill, which provides valuable information on his own battlefield organisation and tactics. He also began making plans for the beautification of Stockholm, and the rebuilding of the royal palace, intended to symbolise absolutism in stone, was one of the first works carried out for him by Tessin in 1715. Was Charles an Enlightened Despot *manqué*, born before his time? In different circumstances would he, as Tessin and others who knew him well believed, have made an excellent peace-time king in the absolutist mould? Perhaps; but it seems unlikely that one who loved war so much could ever have been satisfied by a peaceful life.

In 1713, while still in the Ottoman Empire, Charles ordered a full-scale reorganisation of the Swedish administration. The old colleges were abolished and their place was taken by state departments (*expeditions*), two of which covered foreign affairs and three dealt with military, financial and trade matters. Each department had an *ombudsråd* at its head whose job it was to act as intermediary between the king and the administration. It was part of his responsibility to initiate plans for his department in 'the service of His Majesty and for the benefit of the state'. A sixth department was responsible for seeing that the law of the land was properly observed and that the administration as a whole was fairly carried out. When issues of great general importance arose, all the *ombudsråd* would meet to discuss them with the king. Some reorganisation began at once, although most of it was not carried out until after Charles returned to Sweden at the end of 1714.

(Charles also began to overhaul the unsatisfactory tax system which bore most heavily on the poor. In June 1712 he ordered that in future *all* Swedish subjects must disclose their assets at home and abroad. Salaries and pensions would be exempt but all other money and property would be subject to a percentage tax. New government bodies were set up to deal with the new taxes, which, not surprisingly, were very unpopular with the propertied sector of the population. /

(Many of Charles's other reforms at this time sought to benefit the peasantry. He ordered that farms left derelict by the ravages of the plague should be handed over to wounded or retired soldiers, and that a new land register should be drawn up to ensure greater fairness in the assessment of rents, land taxes and other dues. The work on the new register proceeded slowly as the result of objections by the landowners, and it was not until 1718 that a new single land tax could be introduced.

After Charles's return to Sweden reform proceeded apace. Included among the changes was the introduction of a new calendar to bring the Swedish date system into line with the New Style used in most of Europe, and the introduction in 1718 of a new government post, the first incumbent of which was Tessin, to see that trade and commerce were properly regulated, that hospitals and poorhouses were properly administered and that urban and agricultural problems were properly dealt with.

Charles himself took charge of military and naval reforms. He established a galley-fleet, increased the number of transport ships, including collapsible boats which could be carried over land, and had constructed a fleet of 22 ships of the line by 1718. He ordered the production of quantities of powerful artillery, including rapid-fire field-pieces and heavy siege guns, and arranged for the training of an artillery corps. He began to raise a new army with a proposed operational strength of 60,000, which was organised along modern lines and carefully trained according to Charles's own drill system.

Much of the day-to-day implementation of the domestic reforms was carried out under the supervision of Charles's new minister, the one-eyed Holsteiner, Baron von Görtz. He was officially a diplomat in the service of the Duke of Holstein-Gottorp, but in 1714 he offered his services to Charles whom he greatly admired. He was able and resourceful and he soon took over the whole administration. He rapidly became extremely unpopular, partly because he was a foreigner and partly because of the harsh and ruthless methods he used to obtain the money needed to finance Charles's new army and navy. Most disliked were the heavy taxation and forced loans that he imposed on the more prosperous members of society. In the jockeying for power which took place immediately after Charles's death in 1718, Görtz was arrested and, in what most historians now agree was a miscarriage of justice, he was tried and executed for 'alienating the king's affections from his faithful subjects'.

While it is true that part of the purpose of these domestic reforms was to produce and support a more efficient fighting force, there was also a substantial element of social justice involved. Charles was concerned about ensuring a fairer distribution of the country's economic burden in general and not just about the financing of the war effort. There was opposition and delay in the implementation of some of the reforms. For example, the *riksdag* attempted to revert to the old system of taxation before being overruled by the king. However, the administrative reforms as a whole worked well and in the three years between Charles's return to Sweden and his death a surprising amount was achieved, much of it due to the king's personal involvement and concern.

d) Historians' Views of Charles XII

i) The 'Old School'
In the eighteenth century Charles's reputation in Sweden remained high. He was the revered leader, whose memory was still a living one. If he had failed Sweden in the end, it was only because he had been 'misled' by non-Swedish advisers, such as Görtz, and not through any fault of his own.

By the mid-nineteenth century a more hostile view of Charles was developing among liberal historians who formed what came to be called the 'Old School' of Caroline historiography. They saw him as a warrior-king, who selfishly started the Great Northern War, not because he was attacked by an anti-Swedish coalition, but for personal reasons – the support of his Holstein-Gottorp relations – and who equally selfishly 'ruined his country' by obstinately refusing offers of peace. They concerned themselves with a number of specific problems, in particular the riddle of Charles's death. He had been shot in the head at close range on that November day in 1718 and rumours soon circulated that he had not been killed by a stray enemy ball as officially stated, but had been murdered by someone on his own side. Rumours of this sort were not unusual when a renowned commander died in battle. There had been short-lived rumours of a similar nature after the death of Gustavus Adolphus at Lützen in 1632. However, on this occasion the rumours increased in strength with the passage of time instead of dying down. Suspicion centred on Charles's brother-in-law, Frederick of Hesse-Cassel, as the instigator of a murder plot, for he had most to gain by the king's death (see page 108). On three occasions when Charles's coffin was opened in an attempt to confirm or disprove the rumours of murder no conclusive evidence was ever found. The 'Old School' nevertheless wholeheartedly accepted the murder theory as true, as it conformed with their own liberal beliefs that regicide had been the right, indeed the only, way left to stop an absolutist king and the disasters he was bringing upon Sweden by his irrational behaviour.

Most members of the 'Old School' decided that Charles must have been mad to have acted as he did and, although later research has modified informed historical opinion on the subject of his mental state, the beliefs of the 'Old School' still colour popular western views of Charles. Even today they are occasionally quoted in examination questions based on statements such as, 'All the Vasas were mad, Charles XII more than most'.

ii) The 'New School'
In the last decade of the nineteenth century the 'New School' emerged. Its work was based on research into primary source material and its findings began to answer some of the puzzling questions about Charles's behaviour, which the 'Old School' had dealt with only by accusations of madness.

The 'New School' historians tried, for instance, to show that it would not have been sensible for Charles to have followed up his victory at Narva (1700) with an immediate invasion of Muscovy, as the 'Old School' believed. The Swedes could not leave Augustus and his unbeaten Saxon army in their rear while they went in search of the tsar, or Augustus would have re-invaded Livonia. Charles could not at the time attack Augustus in Saxony because he was forbidden by the terms of his recent treaty with Denmark (1700) from disturbing the peace of the Empire. The only choice open to him was the one he took, to invade Poland and to fight Augustus there (1702–6). It was a rational enough choice given the circumstances, although this is still not accepted as such by all historians (see Chapter 6).

As one historian has written: 'If for the Old School, Charles could do no right, for the New School, he could do no wrong'. Some way had to be found by members of the 'New School' to prove that Charles was not personally to blame for the major disaster at Poltava in 1708. Official archive material for this period is limited, for the papers of the field chancery were sunk in the Dnieper after the battle, on Charles's own orders for security reasons. Nevertheless the 'New School' set out to prove that there were two causes for the defeat – neither of them Charles's fault. Lewenhaupt is made the chief scapegoat, because he failed to arrive at the rendezvous with Charles on time; however, no allowance is made for the particularly wet summer that year and the quagmires which he had to traverse, nor for the fact that a supply train would in any case make much slower progress than the main army. The second excuse offered by the 'New School' is the serious nature of the injury to Charles's foot, together with the resultant high fever from which he was said to be suffering on the day of the battle. Although it is true that he had to be carried on to the field and was unable to lead the army in person, the fever had actually been over for a week. Diaries and journals of the time make it clear that he was not only well enough to have planned the attack, but that he took in person all the decisions for the retreat afterwards.

iii) Modern Research

Further research carried out this century has added to our understanding of Charles XII by modifying many of the earlier findings of both the Old and the New Schools. Lewenhaupt has to some extent been reinstated, particularly over the matter of the surrender of the Swedish army after Poltava. There was certainly some confusion, for which Charles afterwards blamed himself, over the wording of the orders given to Lewenhaupt after the battle. At least one historian is of the opinion that, as a result, the latter honestly if mistakenly believed that, rather than lead his men to meet the king in the Crimea, 'the home of infidel Tartars and Turks', he ought to take the opportunity of surrendering them to a Christian enemy. New light has also been thrown on Charles's strange behaviour after the *kalabalik* (1713) when he retired to bed for nearly a year. The 'Old School' thought this a clear sign of madness; the 'New School' regarded it as a feigned illness, either psychosomatic or consciously assumed for diplomatic purposes. A contemporary French report that Charles had been hurt when he fell after getting tangled up in his spurs during the *kalabalik* was long ignored by historians, but an X-ray of his remains taken in 1917 shows two breaks in an ankle. Modern historical opinion is that it was this injury which kept him laid-up for 10 months.

iv) Conclusion

Charles XII was enigmatic. His motives were often unclear, his aims ambiguous and his actions open to a wide range of historical explanations. Lacking the Vasa fluency of expression, and by nature taciturn, he never made any attempt to justify himself and his actions, either to the people of Sweden or to the rest of Europe. Not surprisingly, therefore, historians find the interpretation of his reign a challenge. Until recently they have ignored his domestic reforms and concentrated almost exclusively on his role in Europe, and therefore on him as a soldier. This has resulted in an incomplete picture of his reign and, to some extent, a misreading of his character, especially in the west where the traditional view of him as a king obsesessed by war persists.

There is not, and appears unlikely to be in the near future, any general concensus of historical opinion on Charles XII. His life and his reign remain subjects for debate and research. Few historians though would now subscribe to the idea of madness to explain everything, as did the Old School, although most would agree that Charles was highly eccentric. The excessive admiration of the New School for whom Charles could do no wrong, has also been replaced by a more balanced view of his career. Modern investigations have thrown new light on some of the more bizarre events of his life, but much is still unexplained and, due to Charles's own silence, may unfortunately remain so.

e) The End of Empire

i) Charles the Man

Charles XII appears austere and unsmiling in his portraits, thin and balding (he wore his own hair instead of the fashionable wig), always in military uniform, a large sabre at his side, and with an indefinable air of what his nineteenth-century British admirers came to call 'the Spartan heroism of his character'. He was the eldest and only one of five sons to survive, and early in life he seems to have adopted a programme to toughen himself. He ignored any weakness and avoided mentioning any illness, such as the malaria from which he suffered during his last year in the Ottoman Empire. He lived simply, eating his meals standing and in silence – and spreading the butter on his bread with his thumbs.

His most abiding characteristic was a singleness of purpose, which to his enemies appeared as obstinacy and to his friends as determination. 'I am resolved', he said in one of the first speeches of his reign, 'never to begin an unrighteous war, but I am also resolved never to finish a righteous one until I have completely humbled my enemies'. He was a courageous and energetic commander in the field and in the early days of the Great Northern War his victories were easily won – perhaps too easily, for he quickly became contemptuous of the enemy. He came to underrate his opponents and, even after the tide turned against him in 1708, to see no reason why he should not completely humble them – given time. Michael Roberts considers that it was Charles XII's 'rigid logic [which] finally condemned the whole imperial structure to ruin' as he was 'drawn step by step to look for one last victory which would put everything right'.

This view can lead, though need not, to the popular belief that he was just a 'war-lord' who 'lost Sweden's great power status because he did not make peace while the going was good'. But that is altogether too simplistic an argument. It does not take into account that there were a number of other factors involved in the loss of the Swedish empire and, so, of great power status – Charles's actions were not the only cause. It does not consider the possibility that continued great power status might not be practicable or desirable for Sweden in the long run and certainly does not envisage the view of Ragnhild Hatton that 'by nearly superhuman efforts of will power and leadership [Charles] propped up the already shaky structure of the empire and prolonged its existence beyond normal expectation'. These and other aspects of the end of the

empire are discussed in the next chapter as part of a general consideration of the Swedish empire and its nature.

ii) The Ruin of his Country?

Swedish research has done much in recent years to destroy the
well-preserved myth that Charles XII 'ruined his country'. The old
belief that Sweden lost 30 per cent of her man power during the war,
becoming 'a land of women and children' by 1718, has been extensively
examined. It is now known that the loss of men as a direct result of
service in the army was comparatively small – not more than 30,000 at
the most. Work on the 1750 census returns show that the number of
men then of an age to have served in Charles's armies was surprisingly
large, and only slightly smaller than the number of women in the same
age group. The old contention that Charles's last army, raised after his
return to Sweden, had to be made up of young boys and old men can no
longer be sustained.

In Sweden and Finland taken together there was a decline in the
general population but it was not large – something between 60,000 and
100,000 out of a total approaching two million. Most of these deaths as
far as Sweden proper was concerned were due to natural causes, a series
of bad harvests, famine and the epidemics of the late 1690s which
followed, and the plague years of 1710–12. The situation in Finland was
rather different and part of the decline there *is* directly attributable to
the war (the Muscovite invasion of 1713).

iii) The Succession

Charles XII never married, although it was at one time generally
expected that he would marry his Danish cousin, Sophie, in accordance
with his parents' wishes, to 'keep the peace between the two countries'.
When pressed to marry 'for the sake of the succession', he replied that
he would do so 'as soon as we get peace', adding that he had to set the
soldiers a good example in sacrificing home life while the war lasted.
His own parents had waited years to marry until the end of the Scanian
War, and it has been suggested that Charles planned similarly to wait
for the end of the Great Northern War. There may have been other
more cogent sexual reasons for his disinclination to marry, but there is
insufficient evidence available to draw any firm conclusions. However,
one historian does suggest that Charles's decision to remain unmarried
was connected with his devotion to his parents' memory, with the high
moral code instilled into him during his harsh upbringing, and with an
emotional attachment to his two sisters.

In the absence of a direct heir, in 1718 there were two contenders for
the throne – Charles's younger sister, Ulrica Eleanor, who had married
Frederick of Hesse-Cassel in 1715, and Charles Frederick of Holstein-
Gottorp, the son of Charles XII's elder sister Hedwig, who had died in
1708 (see the family tree on page 134). Frederick of Hesse-Cassel, who

had been one of Charles XII's close supporters, was strongly opposed to the claims of the Holstein-Gottorp family, for he was ambitious for the throne for himself through his wife. Ulrica, who had a rather better claim at law than the young Duke of Holstein-Gottorp, was also more popular and better prepared to take the throne at her brother's death. However, before she was allowed to do so, she had to agree with the *råd* certain limitations on her prerogative. She then had to submit her case to the *riksdag*, which in 1719 acclaimed her not as hereditary but as *elected* queen, after she had accepted a document abolishing absolutism.

Frederick had already allied himself with the anti-absolutist party in Sweden, and when Ulrica was thought to be asserting her independence overmuch in 1720, she was persuaded to abdicate in his favour. The *riksdag* correctly believed that as he had no hereditary claim of any kind to the throne he was likely to prove more amenable to their wishes than his wife had done. Frederick, who took the title of Frederick I, was forced to agree to yet further diminutions of royal power before his accession was confirmed. These left the *riksdag* in the position of supreme authority and the king as little more than a figurehead.

As a famous Swedish epigram has it:

1 The Glory of the Age is past and gone
  We to our former Nothingness are fated
  King Charles is dead, King Frederick consecrated
  And Sweden's clock has moved from XII to I.

Not only was 1720, as Swedish historians describe, it 'the end of the Age of Greatness and the beginning of the Age of Liberty', but it was also the end of the age of the Vasas. Ulrica and Frederick had no children and the only possible Vasa heir, the Holstein-Gottorp grandson of Charles XII's elder sister, had already been adopted by his aunt the Empress of Russia as her successor before Frederick died in 1751 (see the family tree on page 134). The Swedish succession passed out of the Vasa family after two momentous centuries which had seen the rise and fall of Sweden as a great power.

Making notes on 'Sweden in Decline 1660–1721'

This chapter has two main parts – Charles XI and the growth of absolutism, and Charles XII and the fall of empire – and a short epilogue which deals with the end of absolutism.

The important points to grasp are contained in the answers to the following three two-part questions, which you may like to use as a framework for your notes:

1. How and why was absolutism established in Sweden between 1660 and 1697?
2. How and why was the Swedish empire lost between 1697 and 1721? Note: You will need to add to the 'why' part of this question when you have studied the next chapter.
3. How and why was absolutism toppled in Sweden between 1718 and 1720?

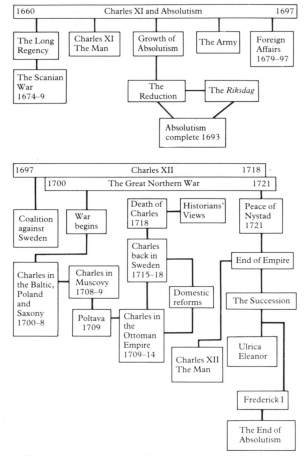

Summary – Sweden in decline 1660–1721

Answering essay questions on 'Sweden in Decline 1660–1721'

You are not very likely to be faced with an essay question on Charles XI, except possibly as one shared with Charles XII. For example:

1. 'Consider whether the work of Charles XII was "a reckless, indeed insane, waste of his father's achievements".'

In answering 'joint' questions of this kind it is important to devote approximately equal attention and space to the two halves of the question. It is often easier to construct an essay plan if you re-word the question first – in this case along the lines, 'What were the achievements of Charles XI? Did Charles XII waste them?'

Charles XII is a perennially popular examination choice, but the range of questions is narrow. The great majority of questions ask, under various guises, whether or not Charles XII was responsible for the end of the empire. Requests for a straightforward narrative do sometimes occur, often in the form of a two-part question:

2. 'Why did Charles XII involve Sweden in war? What were the results?'
3. 'Describe Charles XII's efforts to restore Swedish greatness. Why did he fail?'

More 'open-ended' questions occur also, such as:

4. 'Does Charles XII deserve the verdict that he was "a magnificent failure"?'

There are also occasional questions on his domestic policies:

5. 'How far were Charles XII's domestic reforms the result of Sweden's involvement in the Great Northern War?'

However, 'challenging statements' are by far the most common format. For example:

6. '"Gifted and dedicated, only he could have saved his country's great power position." Consider this view of Charles XII.'
7. '"Inheriting an empire in decline, Charles XII was only able to hasten its collapse." Is this assessment justified?'
8. '"If anyone could have saved the Swedish Empire it was Charles XII." Do you agree with this claim?'
9. '"The decline of Sweden under Charles XII was due to external rather than internal causes." Discuss.'
10. '"The only good service he did his country was his death." Is this a fair comment on Charles XII?'
11. '"Charles XII alone was responsible for the loss of the Swedish empire." Discuss.'

Many of these questions may at first sight seem complicated, especially where they are based on a quotation. However, there is no need to be put off by such questions. There is a simple technique for unlocking the meaning of such a 'challenging statement' type of question. It can be re-phrased and turned round into one or more direct questions. If this were done to question 10 it would become 'Was dying the only good thing Charles XII did for his country?' Once you understand what you are being asked, it is a relatively easy task to plan your essay. Do not forget the last part of a 'challenging statement' question – in this case asking whether the quotation is a fair comment? Your final paragraph should give your conclusions on this point, based on the evidence you have already provided in the rest of the essay. Re-word the remaining questions (6–9 and 11) to make their meaning clearer.

Examiners marking questions on Charles XII almost always expect candidates to display some knowledge of the conflicting views of historians about the end of empire. Did Charles lose the empire for Sweden and, if so, was it his fault? Or did he do his best to save the empire and, if so, why did he fail? This aspect of the topic is discussed further in the next chapter, so you would be well-advised to read it before you attempt to answer any of the questions above.

Source-based questions on 'Sweden in Decline 1660–1721'

1 The Reduction
Read the two short extracts on page 88, and answer the following questions:
a) Explain what is meant by 'retrenchment' (line 6) and 'the king's grace' (line 1). Why is Charles XI described as 'the great royal economist' (line 1)? (4 marks)
b) What is the general tone of the two extracts? Explain your answer. Were the writers justified in taking the line they did? (6 marks)

2 Absolutism
Read the four extracts on pages 89 and 90 and answer the following questions:
a) In the first three extracts (page 89) what is the attitude of the *riksdag* to the king? Explain your answer. To what do they attribute the king's right to absolute power? (6 marks)
b) In the extract on page 90 what does the English visitor believe to have been the reasons for the king's success in pursuit of absolutism? To what extent are the opinions expressed by the visitor i) accurate, and ii) comprehensive? (9 marks)

CHAPTER 6

The Swedish Empire

Although the beginning of the Swedish Empire can be dated soon after 1560 when the sons of Gustav Vasa embarked on a forward foreign policy in the southern Baltic, its real development did not occur until the reign of Gustavus Adolphus 50 years later. It quickly grew to reach its greatest extent and importance in 1660 and as quickly declined. By 1721, nothing remained, apart from a few small possesions in north Germany.

How did the empire come into being? What was its composition? Why did it decline so quickly and completely?

1 The Origins of Empire

In 1611 Sweden did not appear at all a likely candidate for incipient greatness. The country was still backward and poverty stricken compared with many western European countries, particularly France and England. She was poor geographically, with a harsh climate and difficult terrain. She was also poor in manpower. The total population of Sweden–Finland at the beginning of the seventeenth century was probably less than two million, while that of England is estimated to have been about five and a half million, and that of France about sixteen million. She was backward economically. There were still very few towns and no wealthy middle class – the burghers were much the least important of the four estates in the *riksdag*. The country's great natural resources of copper and iron were still largely unexploited, and most trade was still carried on by barter. Taxes as well as rents continued to be paid to the crown in kind, for Sweden remained what she had always been, a largely peasant community of subsistence farmers. She was culturally retarded. The standard of living was low in all classes of society, and only at court had the Renaissance made any impression on the architecture and literature of a country still basically mediaeval in outlook.

However, it can be argued that Sweden was not quite as unsuited to her imperial destiny as her impoverished condition of the early seventeenth century might suggest, for she enjoyed certain domestic strengths that were not immediately apparent. The country was more unified than most other European ones. The king's authority was not restricted by provincial or urban privileges, and nor was it seriously threatened by noble ambitions – Gustav Vasa had seen to that. The church also presented a united front, little troubled by heretical or other divisions. In an age of religious strife, Sweden was monolithically Lutheran – Gustav Vasa had seen to that as well. Her mineral resources held promise for the future and were to transform the country's economy within a few years. Sweden had one other advantage which set her apart from the rest of Europe – her peasantry were represented in the *riksdag* and had a voice in the affairs of state. This gave a firm base to negotiations between king and people and allowed the silver-tongued Vasas to achieve on occasion a national unity of purpose by involving the commonalty, along with the other estates, in support of royal policy. Gustavus Adolphus's farewell to the *riksdag* on the eve of Sweden's entry into the Thirty Years' War is a prime example of this technique. However, Sweden's greatest strength was probably the driving energy, ambition and ability of her Vasa monarchs, all of whom were determined to rule as well as to reign.

a) The Gothic Fantasy

Whether or not early seventeenth century Sweden appeared to outsiders as of little account, the Swedes themselves never doubted their destiny. The Gothic legend, current in Sweden in its earliest form since at least the fourteenth century, had prepared them for a return to past glory. This legend, a strange mish-mash of beliefs, some indigenous, some borrowed, declared that Sweden was the oldest of the nations, having been founded soon after the Flood by Magog. An extraordinary mythical-historical fantasy was built up and elaborated by successive generations of Swedes. Magog's son, Götar, was said to have settled in Uppsala and to have given his name to the Goths, who spread from Sweden over the whole earth and were involved in the siege of Troy, before conquering Rome while the Argonauts were seeking the Golden Fleece in the Baltic and Sweden had become the home of the Amazons. Further additions to the legend identified Sweden with Atlantis, peopled by mighty warriors who taught philosophy to the Ancient Greeks, developed the science of astronomy and produced a great, but sadly, lost literature written in runic characters.

All this and much more was codified in a Latin 'history' of the Goths and Swedes in 1554. The work had a tremendous impact on successive Vasa kings. Eric XIV read it in prison, and Charles IX sponsored an official translation into Swedish. The young Gustavus Adolphus, through his tutor, was deeply influenced by the 'history', and echoes of the Gothic myth appear in some of his speeches to the *riksdag*. Christina saw herself as an Amazon warrior queen, Charles X spoke of leading his Goths to Italy, while Charles XI and Charles XII seemed to embody the virtues of the ascetic, chivalrous Gothic king. Swedish governments from the time of Gustavus Adolphus onwards felt it their duty to sponsor antiquarian research in support of their Gothic past. They carried out investigations into runes and runic inscriptions and undertook excavations of ancient monuments, including sites in Asia Minor, looking for evidence. In 1688 Charles XI issued instructions that:

1 All that redounds to the Swedish and Gothic nation from former
  times may be brought to light, and as it is well known how the
  Goths and Swedes, after their first coming to this country [of
  Sweden] went out again and possessed themselves of new lands
5 and kingdoms both in Asia and Africa, as well as nearer at hand in
  Europe . . . many memorials of them are no doubt to be found in
  Hungary, Austria and the Black Sea, in Thrace, Greece, Italy,
  Switzerland, France and Spain, you are to endeavour to discover
  whether any documentary evidence of them is to be found there.

Young noblemen on the newly fashionable Grand Tour were shown the
'Gothic' buildings of Italy as 'monuments of glories that once had been
[Sweden's], and which in this better time should be again', while
'Gustavus' was hailed as the anagramatic successor to the Roman
Emperor 'Augustus', and as the new hero who would conquer all the
nations of the earth. While a detailed knowledge of the 'Ancient Goths'
was largely confined to the small number of well-educated Swedes,
there is evidence that at least in outline it percolated steadily downwards through society to become part of oral history.
   With this fantastic 'history' behind them, the Swedes were not
surprised to find themselves in possession of an empire in the middle of
the seventeenth century. It was only what they had been expecting.

b) National Pride

Quite apart from the vagaries of the Gothic fantasy, the first half of the
seventeenth century does seem to have been a time of growing pride in
being Swedish as the new, young, independent state found its feet.
There was an interest in studying the Swedish language and literature,
as well as in the country's past. A Vasa style of architecture was
developed and there was even some attempt to create a national
costume. There was also a growing concern for Swedish 'reputation'
and honour in international relations. One of the charges levelled
against the Emperor by Gustavus Adolphus was that Sweden had been
treated with 'scorn and ignominy'. The *riksdag* agreed with the king
that not to provide the necessary money for a war which the Emperor
had made inevitable by his behaviour would bring 'indelible shame and
disgrace' upon Sweden. This fierce new national pride was reinforced at
the peace of Westphalia in 1648 when Sweden achieved great power
status. She was no longer just an insignificant Baltic country but an
important member of the European state system. As Christina said,
when demanding that she be henceforth addressed by the title of
'Majesty', 'Things have much changed in the world since King Gustav
[Vasa] and King Eric [XIV] were in it'.
   However, some historians believe that beneath this new spirit of
national pride there remained an older feeling, not of pride, but of

national inferiority, and that this found expression in a touchy asser-
tiveness and a readiness to take offence which often led Sweden into
conflict. Certainly by the middle of the seventeenth century Sweden's
reputation had become that of a warlike nation, although it is arguable
that this was largely attributable to the character of her sovereigns:
indeed there seems to have been an obvious bellicosity, a love of
fighting for its own sake, in almost all the Vasas. Christina, who once
proposed to lead her troops personally into battle, declared in 1652:

1 Our rise has come through war. It were an eternal disgrace to our
   position and our country if we took no proper care of our
   interests; it would be inexcusable to posterity. Why therefore
   when we see danger and know that God has commanded his
5 people to wage war, why shall we not do it?

Two years later her successor, Charles X, prepared to put into practice
his equally firm belief that 'Sweden's greatness rests on war'. Gustavus
Adolphus and Charles XII would both have agreed with him.

c) The Search for Security

The 'old school' historians, whose views are those most often found in
English language publications, believed that the empire was a reaction
to, and the result of, historical events – encirclement by Denmark,
political instability in the Baltic region (brought about by the collapse of
the Teutonic Knights and the decay of the Hanseatic League), the rise
of Muscovy, and the hostility of both the catholic Vasa kings of Poland
and of the Habsburg Emperor. All these events were interpreted by the
Swedes as threats – actual or potential – to the territorial integrity of
their country whose position in the Baltic was geographically weak.

It was fear, and the resultant need for a suitable response, which led
successive Swedish monarchs and their governments into a 'Search for
Security'. The course they chose was to colonise the trans-Baltic shores
and so produce a series of protective buffer zones against the enemy.
Thus, argues the 'old school', fear of Muscovy led to the incorporation
of Karelia, Estonia, Ingria and Kexholm in order to deny the tsar access
to the Baltic; fear of Denmark led to the incorporation of Bohuslän,
Halland, Skåne and Blekinge in order to deny the Danes control of the
Sound; and fear of Poland led to the incorporation of Livonia in order
to deny Sigismund a possible base from which to invade Sweden. Fear
of the Habsburg Emperor led to Swedish intervention in the Thirty
Years' War and the acquisition of the German lands of Western
Pomerania, Wismar and Bremen-Verden. These lands – carefully
chosen at the peace of Westphalia for their strategic value – acted not
only as buffer zones to frustrate the Habsburgs' 'Baltic Design', but
also formed a defence against Danish expansion as well. Swedish

attempts to control the duchy of Holstein-Gottorp later served a similar anti-Danish purpose.

The 'old school' historians are at pains to point out that, in their opinion, while Swedish foreign policy appeared to outsiders as brutally aggressive, it was in fact mild and defensive. Sweden was not attacking her neighbours or acquiring their territory out of greed, but simply as a minimum response to strategic, financial or other threats posed by those neighbours. War was forced on her by the actions of others. Even Gustavus Adolphus's schemes for a Swedish empire of north Germany were only the end result of his need to defend Sweden from a possible invasion by the Habsburgs and their Polish allies. This fear of invasion by one neighbour or another led to the belief that *dominium maris Baltici* (dominion over the Baltic Sea) was essential to Swedish welfare. Even if it proved necessary to share the dominion with Denmark from time to time, other non-Scandinavian navies must at all costs be kept out of the Baltic. Hence the anger and concern at news of the Habsburg plan to build a Baltic fleet in the late 1620s and Gustavus Adolphus's positive reaction to it.

Was the 'old school' wrong to lay so much emphasis on the search for security as the origin of Sweden's empire? Were there not other factors involved – national pride, personal greed, or, as the 'new school' suggests, an economic struggle for trading rights?

d) Social Causes

Some Swedish historians take a different view of the origins of empire. They argue that its mainspring was social and lay in the greed of the nobility, or in the sufferings of the poor. They consider that the wars of 1630 to 1660 were fought in the selfish interests of one class and 'were a feudal-inspired action to secure their [the nobility's] landed property and shut the mouth of complaining peasants and other troublesome commoners'. For 'a war economy worked to the advantage of the ruling classes, and not only the generals, but also those – the regents, the high aristocracy – who above all found their advantage in an active foreign policy'. It is true that the wars did provide career opportunities in the army, especially for the more ill-educated and impoverished noblemen in the heady days when new territories were being quickly conquered, and war not only 'paid for itself' but provided rich pickings in goods, lands and revenues for those able to profit from it. However, it is equally true that, despite vigorous government war propaganda, there was little general enthusiasm at home for the imperial adventure abroad. Not only among the hard-pressed taxpayers was there dissatisfaction, but also among the nobility many sighed for peace, and felt that the overseas provinces were being too hardly bought and with too little direct advantage to Sweden. Only by the determined forcefulness of

Axel Oxenstierna, for instance, was the *råd* persuaded in 1636 to continue the war in Germany at all.

However, it should be remembered that on no occasion was war initiated at the behest of the Swedish nobility. The final decision was never in their hands. It was in those of the king, often in his alone. In 1621 Gustavus Adolphus decided unilaterally to attack Poland; in 1629–30 he obtained a general agreement from both the *råd* and the *riksdag* to invade Germany, but it was left to him to decide when, how or even if the invasion should take place; Christina did not consult or inform anyone before ordering an attack on Bremen in 1653, and in 1655 Charles X manoeuvred the *råd* into agreeing to a war already made inevitable by his advance mobilisation of the army and its deployment overseas. Therefore the proposition that the empire was created by a privileged class in their own interest does not bear close investigation.

The claim that the mainspring of overseas expansion was 'Swedish poverty' appears equally suspect. The idea that Swedes were driven in large numbers to seek their fortunes outside their homeland in the course of the seventeenth century is not supported by a detailed consideration of the evidence. Most Swedes showed remarkably little desire at any time to leave their 'poverty' and were not much encouraged by their government to do so. For example, they were for some time specifically excluded from colonising Ingria. Swedish governments had to rely heavily on foreign mercenaries to supplement the native standing army and ordinary Swedes were conspicuous by their absence in all the colonies. Any human traffic was actually in the opposite direction. Sweden has been described as an El Dorado by one historian, attracting foreigners who came to fight, to join the administration or to set up as entrepreneurs, and who were quickly absorbed into Swedish society.

e) Economic Motives

Some Swedish historians, members of the 'new school', believe that the motive behind the creation of the Swedish empire was economic rather than political or social, and that it was consciously directed towards obtaining a monopoly of the trade between Muscovy and the West. In its most extreme form this theory was expressed in the contention that 'The attempt to control the Russian market was from beginning to end the alpha and omega of Swedish Baltic policy'.

It is true that since the mid-sixteenth century there had been numerous attempts to funnel trade with Muscovy through Swedish controlled ports but, despite the statements of certain Swedish historians to the contrary, there is no convincing evidence that Gustavus Adolphus or Axel Oxenstierna were motivated to enter the Thirty Years' War by a determination to control this trade. Rather the contrary. In 1621 Gustavus captured the important town and port of

Riga. Although this event was described by one member of the 'new school' as 'one more step on the road towards control of the trade with Muscovy', Gustavus did not see it like that. Within a year, for purely political reasons, he was negotiating to return Riga to Poland. His readiness to give up the city does not suggest that he appreciated or was interested in any of the commercial or financial advantages which the city could – and later, did – provide for Sweden. In the same way, it seems that the Swedish invasion of Prussia in 1626 was important to Gustavus for politico-military reasons rather than economic ones. Although once acquired the Prussian-Polish ports provided, through the tolls, much needed finance for the Swedish invasion of Germany in 1630, their importance to Gustavus always remained strategic. They allowed him to 'keep an open door, both in winter and summer, for free access and withdrawal' of troops along the south Baltic shore.

Soon after Gustavus's death Axel Oxenstierna sent back to Stockholm proposals for a possible alliance with Muscovy, in which he outlined the advantages such an alliance would bring to Sweden. It is revealing that trade was not one of them. When the *riksdag* considered the proposal in detail the following year, trade was the seventh and last advantage they believed would arise from it. On this showing, control of trade with Muscovy does not seem to loom any larger in Swedish foreign policy in the 1630s than it had done in the 1620s.

However, if they do not accord well with the wars of Gustavus Adolphus, the theories of the 'new school' are much more convincing in connection with the expansionist wars of Charles X, whose attack on Denmark in 1658 was as much economic as political. One of its aims was to gain control of both sides of the Sound. This would have given Sweden complete control over Baltic trade with the west, all of which had to pass through the Sound. The Sound tolls themselves would have initially financed the war and afterwards have provided and maintained a fleet strong enough to repel any dissatisfied western nation tempted to contest the Swedish trade monopoly.

f) Conclusions

It is difficult to arrive at any firm conclusions about the motives which led Sweden into her imperial adventure. The most convincing interpretation of the available evidence appears to be a modified 'old school' view. Religious motives appear to have been unimportant even in connection with the Thirty Years' War (see page 56) and while economic and social elements undoubtedly played some part in Swedish expansion – particularly in relation to the earlier Baltic settlements (1560–1632) and to the wars of Charles X (1654–60) – their overall importance appears to have been exaggerated by some historians. The 'search for security' seems on balance to have been the most important single factor involved, especially during the crucial years of 1630–48 which saw Sweden clearly (if temporarily) established as an imperial power.

2 The Nature of the Empire

a) The Colonies

The use of Michael Roberts' words 'Empire' to describe Sweden's expansion in the Baltic region during the seventeenth century, and 'colonies' to describe the individual territories involved, is a convenient and accepted practice and is followed in this book. (Sweden also had one or two short-lived colonial possessions in North America.)

The Swedish empire was widely scattered, its colonies strung out along the shores of the Baltic. This made them difficult to administer from the distant, often ice-bound capital, Stockholm. So, although the empire was comparatively small, it was ill coordinated, and the colonies lacked cohesion. They were populated by Finns, Muscovites, Estonians, Letts, Germans and Danes and their common language, as far as there was one, was German, rather than Swedish. Attempts at colonisation were very limited and Swedes remained a tiny minority of the population in all the provinces. There were, therefore, no strong emotional and national ties between the colonies and the homeland of the kind provided in most empires by a substantial expatriate element in the population.

Historians usually consider the Swedish colonies as falling into three main groups – those acquired from Denmark (Jämtland, Härjedalen, Bohuslän, Skåne, Halland, Blekinge and Gotland), the 'Baltic provinces' (Karelia, Kexholm, Ingria, Estonia and Livonia) and the German lands (Western Pomerania, Wismar and Bremen-Verden). The three groups had little in common, and the individual colonies varied from each other in size and wealth. This made it difficult to follow the principle of government laid down in the early days of the empire that all provinces should be financially self-supporting. The only obvious bond uniting the empire was religion. Apart from Ingria (which was Orthodox), all the colonies were Lutheran like Sweden.

Given the incoherent nature of the empire, how far was Sweden able to administer it effectively? There was no single constitutional tradition or practice covering the whole empire and no supreme council exercised overall authority. Although the *råd* did from time to time discuss imperial affairs, it was very rare for the *riksdag* to do so. This lack of concern with the empire was not surprising. In 1634 the 'Form of Government' had effectively debarred representatives from the Baltic or German lands by declaring that only persons ordinarily resident in mainland Sweden–Finland could be members of either body. Neither *råd* nor *riksdag* therefore felt any particular interest in colonial problems. In Stockholm the colonies were looked after, if at all, only by special sections of the Chancery, and by the Treasury which simply drew up detailed budgets and left the provinces to do the best they could to raise them.

i) The Danish colonies

These were never really colonies in the accepted sense of the word. Very similar in culture and background to Sweden herself, it was very probable that, for geographic if for no other reasons, they would sooner or later have been incorporated into Sweden. Nevertheless their 'Swedification' presented more problems to the Stockholm government than might have been expected. The strategic importance of the southern provinces of Skåne, Blekinge, Halland and Bohuslän, and the danger that even after their formal cession to Sweden in 1660–1, Denmark might try to recover them meant that they must be encouraged to become Swedish. In 1662 they were given the right to representation in the *riksdag* and the *råd*, but were otherwise little affected by their union with Sweden. Until 1679, for instance, Danish law remained in force and Danish clergy conducted services in their own language. But the Scanian war changed everything. There were outbreaks of anti-Swedish revolt among former Danish subjects during it, and a much more drastic programme of 'de-nationalisation' was instituted at its end. Swedish settlers were encouraged to move into the southern provinces, a new all-Swedish town was built and measures were taken to drive out pro-Danish rebels still in hiding. The right to representation in the *riksdag* was withdrawn and only restored when new 'Swedifying' measures were agreed. Swedish law, language and church organisation were gradually introduced so that by 1700 the Danish provinces were fully and permanently integrated into Sweden. Their loyalty was certain enough for cavalry regiments from Skåne to be employed alongside native Swedish troops in Charles XII's army during the Great Northern War.

ii) The Baltic Colonies

Sweden's influence was most strongly felt in the Baltic lands, where at the time of their acquisition by Sweden life was brutish beyond belief. War, ignorance, hunger, oppression and servitude was the lot of the peasants at the hands of a barbarous, German-speaking rural nobility and a degraded, uncaring church, many of whose parishioners had reverted to paganism. Gustavus Adolphus was among those Swedes who regarded the situation with horror. A commission was sent into Livonia and Estonia in 1627 and, in spite of the objections of the Baltic nobility, changes began to be made. Slowly the church was reformed, the judicial system was improved, and above all some education was made available. One of Gustavus's last acts in November 1632 was to establish and endow the new university at Dorpat. Agriculture and trade also benefited from Swedish intervention. However, serfdom was not eradicated. This was because those Swedes who, like Axel Oxen-stierna, received large grants of land – he owned one eighth of Livonia – soon sank their principles, and adapted themselves to the ways of the Baltic nobility. Serfdom continued unchecked.

With the Reduction of the l680s and the return of most of the land into the king's hands, the Swedish government could begin a series of social reforms. An extended programme of primary education was instituted by Charles XI and by the end of his reign every parish in Livonia had a school of some sort, the Bible had been translated into Lettish, and the University of Dorpat, which had recently fallen on hard times, had been re-founded. Charles himself wanted to abolish serfdom, but he was only able to ensure that on crown lands it came to an unofficial end. Elsewhere it continued as before. Swedish law was gradually introduced into all the Baltic provinces, and in 1686 torture was prohibited in Estonia (as it already was in the rest of the empire). By 1700, although much remained to be done, some degree of civilisation had been brought to the Baltic colonies. However, it was not to last long, and Peter the Great's conquests quickly returned the Baltic people to their earlier state of degradation and servitude.

iii) The German Colonies

In the German provinces of Pomerania and Bremen-Verden, the king ruled only as duke and his authority was restricted by pre-existing constitutional and legal practices. This was so much the case that Charles XI on one occasion complained that the Pomeranians acted 'as though they were not our subjects but a separate republic with which we are obliged formally to negotiate'. The peace of Westphalia had left Sweden with little room for manoeuvre in her German territories. Both Pomerania and Bremen-Verden remained part of the Holy Roman Empire; their law was that of the Empire – no question of Swedification here. They retained their estates, their own civil service and German remained the language of government, except in the Pomeranian treasury run by Stockholm-trained staff, where Swedish was spoken. By and large, both Pomerania and Bremen-Verden managed their own affairs with very little reference to Stockholm. Legislation and taxation was organised by the estates, and royal ordinances were issued in the name of the duke not of the king of Sweden.

Generally speaking, relations between the king and his German colonies were good and government was carried on in a spirit of cooperation. In 1663 both duchies received new constitutions by which the duke agreed to rule only through the estates and to levy civil taxes only with their consent, so laying the foundations of an administration which was to long outlast Swedish rule.

While the empire remained to the end a series of separate colonies only loosely connected together, and with no clear imperial ethos, there was never any nationalist opposition to Swedish rule (apart from the short outburst in the former Danish provinces during the Scanian War). There is even some evidence that the Pomeranians, for instance, quickly came to think of themselves as Swedes. As Michael Roberts remarked, 'Whatever else the empire was, it was not a collection of oppressed peoples rightly struggling to be free'. Nationalist uprisings played no part in its end.

b) Imperial Economics

Apart from a reasonably willing acceptance of Swedish rule, there were certain other unifying forces at work within the empire, linking the colonies with one another and with Sweden. One of these forces had always been religion. In the same way that Sweden herself was uniformly Lutheran so, with the exception of Ingria, was the empire. However, by the end of the century economics had become a much stronger link than religion.

While economic motives played little part in Sweden's entry into the Thirty Years' War, once it was over Axel Oxenstierna was fully aware of the commercial opportunities which the colonies offered. The College of Commerce, which he set up in 1651, was an exceptional government department in that it made an attempt to look at imperial policy as a whole. The aim of the College was to encourage the development of the empire as a single trading body able to exploit the favourable middleman position of Sweden and her colonies. Some progress in the development of foreign trade was made, and by the end of the century a respectable merchant fleet had been built up. Despite the absence of internal tariff barriers, trade between Sweden and her colonies was minimal until the 1690s when, as the result of a series of bad harvests, there was famine in Sweden. Consignments of grain from the Baltic and German provinces became vital and in 1696 alone 800,000 tons reached Sweden (three times as much as 20 years before). The provinces had suddenly become economically important: they had become Sweden's granary.

The Reduction of Charles XI revolutionised the financial situation in the empire as a whole. In the provinces as much as five-sixths of the land had been alienated, and it was now restored to the crown. The old problem of how to make the colonies self-sufficient disappeared. They not only became self-supporting, but they produced an annual surplus for the Treasury in Stockholm. By the end of the seventeenth century the empire was operating at a profit for the first time in its history. There was enough money to fill the Treasury and finance Charles XI's new army. Administratively too new developments were taking place.

With royal control re-established over the greater part of the land, the king could exercise his will in the provinces as unquestionably as in Sweden. In 1686, for instance, the Ecclesiastical Law was imposed, by royal authority, throughout the whole empire.

Economic, political and administrative bonds were thus being forged in the last few years of Charles XI's reign to unite the empire as never before.

3 The End of Empire

Historians find themselves in disagreement over almost every aspect of the Swedish empire from beginning to end. They debate whether Gustavus Adolphus and Charles X were right to acquire the empire at all – was it in Sweden's interest to do so? Could she have become a great power in any other way? They also debate the reasons for its loss. Was it inevitable? Was it the fault of Charles XII? The evidence is far from clear on any of these questions.

If Sweden's empire was substantially acquired in a search for security, did it fulfil its purpose? Some historians believe that, as far as the German territories were concerned, it generally did not. They suggest that the possession of Pomerania and Bremen-Verden made Sweden more, rather than less, vulnerable, opening up the unwelcome possibility (as happened in 1659) of war on three fronts. The German possessions were very open to attack and were difficult, and therefore expensive, to defend whether by land or sea. In 1658 Charles X estimated that Pomerania required 8,000 troops to defend it in peace and 17,000 in war. This was because it had poor natural defences, and therefore required substantial and costly fortifications to protect its long and exposed land frontiers. Along with Bremen, it was very cut off from Sweden, dependent on the navy for communications with Stockholm and for reinforcements and supplies. These could take seven months or even longer in winter to arrive, whereas the Baltic lands were much more accessible – if necessary they could be reached from Sweden by an overland route-march via Finland.

Gustav Adolphus's successors were obsessed by the danger of attack by Denmark or the Habsburgs. Even in the later seventeenth century, when Habsburg power had faded and the Danish threat had receded, Swedish governments continued to concentrate their military resources on defence of the German provinces and of southern Sweden to the detriment of the Baltic lands. Here many of the fortifications had either passed into private hands or had fallen into ruins by the 1690s, and garrisons had been reduced to provide more troops for Germany. Charles XI ignored the growing strength of Muscovy, the old enemy in the east, until too late, and the ill-protected Baltic provinces were to be overrun within a few years of his death by Peter the Great. It is ironic that the loss of the German provinces, on which so much care had been lavished, proved comparatively unimportant. Their day of usefulness to Sweden was over. Their loss, by the time it came, was less a strategic disaster than a blow to national pride.

One historian has suggested that if Sweden had not been 'enticed' into the Thirty Years' War and diverted by the need to protect her German gains, she would have been able to cope with Muscovy, retain the Baltic lands and become a great power. (There is of course the other argument that Sweden only became a great power because she *did* become involved in Germany. Supporters of this theory point out that the new German possessions provided the bases from which to defeat Denmark and enabled Sweden to reach her natural frontiers.) However, historians are, generally speaking, undecided whether Sweden would in fact have been able to hold back the growing power of Muscovy and its ten million inhabitants from the Baltic for any length of time. On balance it seems most likely that Muscovy would sooner or later, by sheer force of numbers and by virtue of her much greater resources, have succeeded in reaching the sea whatever measures Sweden had taken to prevent it. That is not to say that by careful attention to the defence of the Baltic lands the evil day might not have been postponed for a considerable time.

a) Charles XII to Blame?

The end of empire is most often blamed directly on Charles XII and his 'blinkered obstinacy' in refusing on more than one occasion to make peace when the opportunity arose during the Great Northern War. However, not all historians agree with this view. Ragnhild Hatton, Charles XII's biographer and apologist, believes that he did all he could to preserve the empire and 'did it very well':

1 If anyone could have saved Sweden's great power position he would have been the man, with his gifts as a commander, with his capacity for inspiring loyalty in his maturity, and with his dedication to the task fate had allotted to him.

Elsewhere, though, even she admits that it may have been an 'obsession with his duty of defending and maintaining the original position' of Sweden as a great power which drove him, perhaps wrongly, to fight on after others would have surrendered.

He inherited from his father the strongest army (90,000 well-armed and highly trained men) and navy (34 ships of the line and 11 frigates) Sweden had ever seen, but they were maintained by an economy firmly based on a policy of continued peace and neutrality. The army was never intended to serve outside Swedish territory, never meant to be led into Poland and Saxony or into Muscovy. One Swedish historian has pointed out that if Charles had used his father's military provision as it was intended to be used, all would probably have gone very differently. But this he was not willing to do. Although the Great Northern War began for the Swedes as a defensive war against attack by the coalition, it was developed by Charles into an offensive one, taking the army further and further afield until most of it was lost at Poltava.

It is probably accurate to claim that much, perhaps the major part, of the blame for the end of the empire must fall on Charles XI and his predecessors who neglected the Baltic lands over the years, and on Charles XII who finally lost them, so allowing Muscovy to gain access to the sea. It was the change in the balance of power in the Baltic which resulted, and the arrival of a Muscovite fleet in the 'Swedish Lake' after 1710, which meant that the break-up of the Swedish empire became only a matter of time. Whatever the ploys and plots being hatched by Charles in the Ottoman empire between 1709 and 1714, or the struggles of the government in Stockholm, there was little they could do militarily or diplomatically to alter the situation. They could only postpone the inevitable. Perhaps it was as well for him that Charles did not live to see the end of the war and Sweden's final humiliation in the treaty of Nystad.

It is also probably reasonable to maintain that some further blame must be attributed to Charles XII personally for his conduct of the war. Whether he had been wise or unwise to spend the years 1702–7 chasing round Poland and Saxony, he was still in a position of strength in 1708. If he had then been content to recover Peter's Baltic conquests and to use them as a base for a limited invasion of Muscovy, instead of pursuing his dream of a 'radical solution' (all out victory and a dictated peace) by a march on Moscow, the disasters which followed might well have been averted. The military decisions of the war were taken by Charles, and by him alone. If the glory of Narva was his, so too was the shame of Poltava.

b) Importance of External Factors?

What about external factors? How significant are they in the loss of the empire?

Oxenstierna realised at the end of the Thirty Years' War that Sweden owed her success at that time to an exceptional state of international affairs – to the temporary weakness of her neighbours, Germany, Poland, Muscovy and Denmark. There was no power strong enough to contest Swedish domination of the Baltic in the middle of the seventeenth century.

Half a century later the situation was much less favourable to Sweden, who was surrounded at the beginning of Charles XII's reign by jealous neighbours whose enmity she had aroused in the process of acquiring her empire. In Germany there was growing resentment among the princes, including the Emperor, at Sweden's continued presence in the Empire, and a strong wish to overturn the 1648 settlement. The election of the war-like and ambitious Augustus, Elector of Saxony, as king of Poland in 1697 rightly caused particular concern to Sweden, for his ambitions in Livonia led him into alliance with Muscovy in 1699. The anti-Swedish coalition was completed by Sweden's old rival, Denmark. Relations between the two Scandinavian countries had remained strained after the Scanian War, when Denmark, although the victor, had gained nothing from the peace settlement. In addition, the issue of who controlled Holstein-Gottorp was still unresolved.

Denmark, Saxony–Poland and Muscovy were thus actively ranged against Sweden by the beginning of 1700 – while Brandenburg–Prussia (Denmark's ally in the Scanian War) and other German states threatened from the side-lines. It was a formidable array which confronted the young Charles XII on all sides. Possibly it was his youth – he was only 18-years-old – and his comparative inexperience which encouraged his enemies to move in quickly and to attack on three fronts. He had no choice but to fight. For once it was true to say that Sweden had had war forced upon her. The Great Northern War was not initially of Charles's making – even if, as his detractors argue, its prolongation was.

Perhaps instead of asking, as historians normally do, why Charles after a brilliant start eventually lost the war, it would be worth considering why Muscovy came out of the war as the overall winner. The answer lies partly in Muscovy's enormous resources of men and materials, but much more in the personality, drive, energy and ability of the tsar, Peter the Great. After his early defeat at Narva he built up, re-organised and re-equipped his army into the powerful fighting force which destroyed the Swedes at Poltava. He also developed his naval power – essential for dealing with a maritime empire such as Sweden's once he had gained access to the sea. In 1710 he had no warships in the Baltic. At the end of the war his fleet was larger than that of either Denmark or Sweden. Muscovy had replaced Sweden as the dominant power in the Baltic, and most of the credit for doing so must go to Peter the Great in person.

c) Conclusion

It seems probable that the Swedish empire was doomed once the Baltic provinces fell to Peter the Great and allowed him access to the sea. They were lost because of Swedish neglect over a long period of time and because of the military superiority of Muscovy. It is a matter for debate how far Charles XII was responsible for their final loss by leaving them inadequately defended in 1702 when he invaded first Poland and afterwards Muscovy. To go further than this in apportioning responsibility is to enter the realm of imponderables and to go round in circles – If the coalition had not been formed against Sweden, if Charles had not been so obstinate, if he had made peace when the tsar offered. . . The possibilities are endless.

d) The Empire in Sweden's Interest?

Whether the empire was ever in Sweden's interest is debatable. In the early days, although Sweden was never bankrupt, it put a financial strain on the country; it enmeshed Sweden in affairs beyond the Baltic and aroused the jealous enmity of her neighbours; except at the beginning it did not provide her with security; it involved her in expensive wars. What did she gain? Great power status, national prestige as co-guarantor of the treaty of Westphalia and, the only lasting gain, the achievement of her natural boundaries.

Modern Swedes seem to feel a sense of guilt that their country was ever an imperial power and to consider that it was just as well the empire lasted no longer than it did. This may have something to do with the contrast between the Age of Greatness and the so-called Age of Liberty which followed, a time of cultural flowering amidst a series of liberalising constitutional developments. What contemporary Swedes thought about the collapse of their empire is not known for certain, but it may be, as many historians believe, that it was with a sense of relief that they laid down the burden of an empire in which they had never had a great deal of interest, and of which they were tired by 1721.

Making notes on 'The Swedish Empire'

This chapter attempts to sum-up much that you have studied in chapters 3, 4 and 5. It should enable you i) to clarify your ideas on why the Swedish empire was acquired, ii) to understand the significant features of its constituent parts, and iii) to gain an understanding of the arguments surrounding its demise. In particular, it is to be hoped that you will be able to develop coherent views about the extent to which Charles XII was to blame for the loss of the empire.

Your notes need not be detailed. It should be sufficient just to jot down a series of points in answer to the following questions:

1. What were the motives or aims of Gustavus Adolphus and his successors in acquiring an empire for Sweden?
2. What were the similarities and differences between the three groups of colonies making up the empire?
3. Why was the Swedish empire lost?

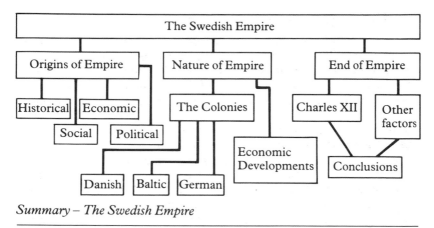

Summary – The Swedish Empire

Answering general essay questions on 'Sweden and the Baltic 1523–1721'

You will find some sample general essay questions on Sweden at the end of chapter 1 (pages 12–13). Further examples are:

1. 'Why had Sweden failed to maintain her great power status by the end of the period 1660–1721?'
2. 'When in the seventeenth century was Sweden at the height of her power? How and why did it decline?'
3. 'Had Sweden ceased to dominate the Baltic by 1679?'
4. 'How far was Sweden "the overlord of the Baltic" between 1648 and 1721?'
5. 'How well established was Sweden as a Baltic power by the early seventeenth century?'

Very few general questions on this topic cover the sixteenth or early seventeenth centuries. Nearly all are concerned with the period from the Thirty Years' War to the Peace of Nystad and each question covers not only a long span of time, but also a great deal of history. Even more than for any other type of question, therefore, it is important to spend time thinking before you write. Otherwise, there is a real danger that you will attempt to cram too much detail into your answer and will run out of time. You will need to be very selective when deciding what to include.

Begin by making sure that you understand what the examiner is asking. Do this by re-writing the question in your own words. Be careful to double-check the beginning and end dates of the period to be covered by your answer. Next, compile a list of points you wish to make, arranging them in whatever order seems best – most important first, least important first – or according to some other criterion which seems to you appropriate – such as military, economic, political or religious. In your final paragraph you need to make clear the significance of the arrangement you have chosen.

Source-based questions on 'The Swedish Empire'

1 National Pride
Read the extracts on pages 115 and 116. Answer the following questions:
a) Explain what is meant by 'all that redounds to the Swedish and Gothic nation' (page 115, line 1) and 'inexcusable to posterity' (page 116, line 3). (4 marks)
b) What phrase in the first extract shows Charles XI's commitment to the Gothic fantasy? Why did successive generations of Swedes find it such an attractive belief? (4 marks)
c) The second extract contains a number of sweeping statements made by Christina about Sweden and war. What are they? Which, if any, are correct? Explain your choice. (6 marks)
d) What light does the second extract throw on the character of Christina? How far is it consistent with what else you know of her? (6 marks)

Further Reading

Two 'easy reading' histories of Sweden, which present the differing views of two modern historians, one British and the other Swedish, are:

Stewart Oakley, *The Story of Sweden* (Faber, 1966)

This is too condensed and superficial in its treatment of the sixteenth and seventeenth centuries to be any more than a brief introduction to the period (Chapters 6 to 10 are relevant).

Ingvar Andersson, *A History of Sweden* (Weidenfeld and Nicolson, 1970 2nd edition)

This well illustrated volume is by a representative of the 'New School' of Swedish historians. First published in 1940, it is still a useful starting point and is worth a quick read through of the relevant sections (Chapters 12–23).

Michael Roberts is by far the most prolific and notable writer in English on Swedish history. Particularly recommended among his many volumes are:

Michael Roberts, *The Early Vasas* (Cambridge University Press Paperback, 1986)

This is a very detailed account of the Vasa kings from 1523 to 1611.

Michael Roberts, *The Swedish Imperial Experience 1560–1718* (Cambridge University Press Paperback, 1984)

Do not be misled by the brevity of this book. It is packed full of thought-provoking comments, but does pre-suppose a reasonable knowledge of the events of the period under discussion. It is not a straightforward history and is not a book to start with.

Michael Roberts, *Gustavus Adolphus and the Rise of Sweden* (English University Press, 1973)

The introduction is particularly useful.

Gustavus Adolphus's part in the Thirty Years' War is also considered at some length in:

Geoffrey Parker (ed), *The Thirty Years' War* (Weidenfeld and Nicolson, 1984)

An older view of Gustavus Adolphus's activities can be found in:

C. V. Wedgwood, *The Thirty Years' War* (Cape, 1938)

Ragnhild Hatton, *Charles XII* (Historical Association pamphlet, 1984)

This is a condensation of her mammoth biography, and provides an excellent introduction to the historical arguments surrounding the reign.

Voltaire, *Charles XII* (in numerous translations, including Everyman)

This is a splendidly biased heroic story, often decried as a 'fairy-tale', but still worth reading for its near contemporaneity.

Among other biographies of the period, recommended is:

Georgina Masson, *Queen Christina* (Secker and Warburg, 1968) ✓

This is a very readable, non-sensationalised account of a strange career.

A general history of the Baltic region is:

D. Kirby, *The Baltic World 1492–1772* (Longman, 1990) ✓

This concentrates on socio-economic themes, and although it has only limited direct relevance to Sweden, it may be of interest to the general reader.

Acknowledgements

The Publishers would like to thank the following for permission to reproduce material in this volume:
Cambridge University Press, for the extract from *Gustavus Adolphus and the Rise of Sweden* by M. Roberts (1973).

The Publishers would also like to thank the following for their permission to use copyright illustrations:
Kungl.Biblioteket, Stockholm p. 41; Livrustkammaren, Stockholm cover; National Museum, Stockholm pp. 15, 43, 50, 93.

Every effort has been made to trace and acknowledge ownership of copyright. The Publishers will be glad to make suitable arrangements with any copyright holders whom it has not been possible to contact.

Glossary

These are the Swedish words most commonly used in the text:

frälse (literally 'deliverance') i.e. free, exempt – usually exempt from taxation, a privilege of the nobility. Came therefore also to mean 'noble' or 'belonging to a noble' e.g. frälsejord, land belonging to a noble, or frälsebonde, peasant belonging to a noble.

ofrälse not exempt from taxation, i.e. non-noble

råd (officially the riksrad) – Council of the Realm; *med råds råde*, with the Council's counsel, i.e. with the Council's advice

rik the state

riksdag the estates, the diet, the parliament (cf. Reichstag)

Proper Names

Generally in this book English forms of proper names have been used e.g. Charles XII not Karl XII, Christina not Kristina, and Gustavus Adolphus not Gustav II Adolf.

Place names have usually been left in their Swedish form. Sometimes though where the English form is also commonly met with, it is on the first occasion put alongside e.g. Skåne (Scania), Göteborg (Gothenburg).

Pronunciation

Below is given an approximate guide to some of the more un-English sounds found in Swedish:

å like *aw* in l*aw* e.g. råd = rawd,

ä usually like *e* in p*e*t e.g. Strängnäs = Strengness

ö like *er* without sounding the *r*

g before e, i, y, ä, ö like *y* in *y*et e.g. Västergötland = Vesterye(r)tland; before all other letters as *g* in *g*et, e.g. Gotland

j like *y* in *y*et e.g. Jämtland = Yemtland

k before e, i, y, ä, ö like *ch* in *ch*urch

sk before e, i, y, ä, o like *sh* in *sh*ore
before a, o, u å like *sk* in *sk*ate e.g. Skåne = Skawne

sj, skj, sti, stj always like *sh* e.g. Oxenstierna = Oxenshtierna

w like *v*

y like a short *i* e.g. Nystad = Nistad

Genealogical Table

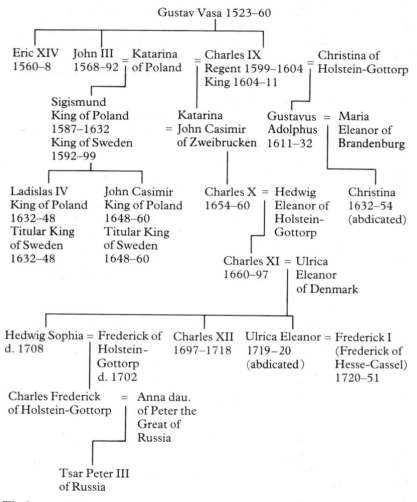

Gustav Vasa 1523–60

Eric XIV
1560–8

John III
1568–92
= Katarina
of Poland

Charles IX
Regent 1599–1604
King 1604–11
= Christina of
Holstein-Gottorp

Sigismund
King of Poland
1587–1632
King of Sweden
1592–99

Katarina
= John Casimir
of Zweibrucken

Gustavus
Adolphus
1611–32
= Maria
Eleanor of
Brandenburg

Ladislas IV
King of Poland
1632–48
Titular King
of Sweden
1632–48

John Casimir
King of Poland
1648–60
Titular King
of Sweden
1648–60

Charles X
1654–60
= Hedwig
Eleanor of
Holstein-
Gottorp

Christina
1632–54
(abdicated)

Charles XI = Ulrica
1660–97   Eleanor
of Denmark

Hedwig Sophia
d. 1708
= Frederick of
Holstein-
Gottorp
d. 1702

Charles XII
1697–1718

Ulrica Eleanor
1719–20
(abdicated)
= Frederick I
(Frederick of
Hesse-Cassel)
1720–51

Charles Frederick
of Holstein-Gottorp
= Anna dau.
of Peter the
Great of
Russia

Tsar Peter III
of Russia

The house of Vasa

Chronological Table

1518	Unsuccessful invasion of Sweden by Denmark during which Gustav Vasa taken to Denmark as hostage.
1520	Successful invasion of Sweden by Denmark – escape of Gustav Vasa and return to Sweden in disguise.
1520	November, Bloodbath of Stockholm.
1522	Most of Sweden and Finland came under control of Gustav Vasa as leader of anti-Danish movement.
1523	June, Gustav Vasa, aged about 24, elected king of Sweden, begins campaign to make the church pay towards government expenses. Lutheran doctrines reach Sweden.
1525	Revolt in Dalarna suppressed.
1526	First Lutheran texts in Swedish published.
1527	Revolt of the *Daljunkare* suppressed. June, meeting of the *riksdag* held at Västerås to discuss future of the church. By the Recess of Västerås power of the bishops destroyed and the church brought under royal control for political and financial reasons, not for doctrinal ones.
1531	Laurentius Petri's consecration as Archbishop of Uppsala marked official break with Rome. 'Church-bell' revolt in Dalarna.
1534/7	War with Lübeck.
1538	Conrad Pyhy's arrival in Sweden. Appointed Chancellor.
1540	Church made into a state department with appointment of *superattendants*. Monarchy made hereditary in Vasa family.
1541	First complete translation of Bible into Swedish.
1542	Nils Dackes's revolt.
1543	Fall of Pyhy.
1544	Succession Pact further extended principle of hereditary monarchy. King now supreme in church and state.
1554/7	War with Muscovy.
1560	September, death of Gustav Vasa.
1560/9	Eric XIV.
1569/92	John III.
1592/1604	Sigismund (king of Poland 1587–1632).
1599/1604	Civil war in Sweden.
1604/11	Charles IX.
1611	November, Gustavus Adolphus (born December, 1594) became king.
1612	January, Accession Charter curbed royal power. Axel Oxenstierna appointed Chancellor (he held this post for 42 years until his death in 1654).

1614/15	Judicature Ordinances reformed legal system.
1618	Exchequer Ordinance reformed Treasury. Chancery Ordinance reformed Chancery.
1620	Reforms of army and navy begun.
1621	Invasion of Livonia and capture of Riga by Gustavus.
1623	First *Gymnasium* set up to improve education.
1625	Rest of Livonia conquered.
1626	Swedish invasion of Prussia.
1627	Swedish fears of 'Habsburg Design' in the Baltic.
1629	Valuable Prussian and Polish port tolls acquired by Sweden.
1630	June, Gustavus landed at Peenemünde and began Swedish intervention in the Thirty Years' War.
1631	Franco-Swedish treaty signed. Protestant city of Magdeburg sacked by Imperial troops. Swedish victory at Breitenfeld gave Gustavus control of half of Germany by end of the year.
1632	Swedish plans for a German Protestant League drawn up. November, Gustavus killed at Lützen leaving only a six-year-old daughter, Christina.
1632/44	Regency headed by Oxenstierna, who also took charge of Swedish affairs in Germany.
1633	League of Heilbronn formed.
1634	Swedish army defeated at Nördlingen.
1635	Surrender of port tolls as price of 26 year truce with Poland led to financial difficulties.
1638	Franco-Swedish treaty committed Sweden to fight alongside France for three years in return for financial help.
1641	Franco-Swedish treaty renewed for duration of the war.
1643/5	Successful Swedish invasion of Denmark.
1644	Christina came of age.
1648	Peace of Westphalia gave Sweden possessions in Germany and established her as a great power.
1650	Peasant unrest over alienation came to a head at the *riksdag*.
1651	Christina attempted to abdicate in favour of her cousin Charles Gustavus.
1654	The *råd* finally agreed to her abdication.
1654	Charles X became king. Death of Oxenstierna.
1655	Charles agreed to a partial Reduction. War with Poland, Brandenburg and Denmark.
1658	Former Danish provinces of Halland, Skåne and Blekinge ceded to Sweden.
1660	Death of Charles X. Sweden at height of imperial power.
1660/72	The Long Regency.
1674/9	The Scanian War – Sweden defeated – rescued by France.

1680	The Regents called to account over irregularities.
1682	Major Reduction begun under king's direct control. The great magnates claimed to be ruined financially. Their political power reduced.
1682/93	The *riksdag* agreed to series of resolutions giving Charles absolute power.
1697	Death of Charles XI. Accession of Charles XII. Although only 15-years-old, declared of full age and given absolute power.
1697/9	Formation of anti-Swedish coalition of Muscovy, Poland–Saxony and Denmark.
1700	Great Northern War began.
1700/2	Charles XII successful in Ingria, Livonia and Courland.
1702/6	Charles XII successful in Poland.
1708/9	Charles XII unsuccessful in Muscovy. Defeated at Poltava.
1709/10	Sweden's Baltic possessions lost. Swedish influence in Poland at an end.
1709/14	Charles XII in the Ottoman empire.
1712–16	Sweden's German possessions lost. Most of Finland occupied by Muscovy.
1712	Swedish tax system overhauled.
1713	Swedish administration reorganised.
1714	Charles XII at Stralsund. Baron Görtz appointed chief minister.
1715	Charles XII back in Sweden.
1718	November, Charles XII killed while besieging a Danish fortress in Norway.
1719	Charles XII succeeded by younger sister, Ulrica Eleanor, as elected queen.
1720	Ulrica Eleanor abdicated in favour of husband, Frederick.
1721	Treaty of Nystad brought Great Northern War to an end. Finland, Wismar, and part of Pomerania restored to Sweden – rest of Empire remained lost.

Index

Readers seeking a specific piece of information might find it helpful to consult the table of *Contents* and the *Chronological Table* as well as this brief *Index*.